How to get the most out of life

How to get the most out of life

The ABC of a negotiator

By Arthur M. Rolls

Disclaimer
Some characters and events in this book are fictitious. Any similarity to real persons, living or dead, is coincidental and not intended by the author.

Dedicatie speciala pentru micuta lui Arthur

La multi ani scumpiiiiiiiiiiiiiiiiiiiii !!!

Stiu ca ti-am promis de mult un exemplar din aceasta carticica, insa m-am gandit ca daca tot o sa iti ofer unul, o sa fie unul unic, pentru o ocazie unica. Ei bine, aceasta ocazie unica a venit, si sincer nu cred ca exista una mai potrivita, deoarece astazi s-a nascut cea mai minunata persoana din lume (*adica tu, de tine e vorba Biut*).

M-am gandit mult mult mult la tine zilele astea (*bine, recunosc, in general, dar mai ales zilele astea*) si la cat esti de adorabila si scumpica si minunata, insa tu stii deja toate lucrurile astea pentru ca spre deosebire de toate celelalte cupluri naspa noi ne aratam destul de des afectiunea. Totusi, tinand cont ca tu n-ai mai scris in mini-jurnalele tale dragute (*btw – awff sunt partea cea mai mare*) nimic inca de anul trecut, m-am gandit ca ar putea fi util sa consemnez aici doar cateva dintre momentele noastre putin mai speciale (*oricum toate momentele cand suntem amandoi sunt speciale*). Bineinteles, nu pot mentiona „momente speciale" fara sa-l mentionez pe cel in care ne-am cunoscut (*God bless taberele in Grecia*). Recunosc, cand te-am vazut prima data, tiganca si cu ochelarii aia dragu, deoarece erai nu doar cea mai frumoasa fata din tabara aia, dar si cea mai inteligenta, venita cu biletu ala de copii destepti, nu imi faceam mari sperante, eu care ajunsesem acolo Dumnezeu stie cum. Ei bine, se pare ca am avut noroooc. Si am stiut ca am noroc. Am stiut de cand inghetam amandoi in piscina, de cand faceam poze pe vaporas, chiar de cand ne-am tinut prima data de mana cand ne intorceam de la plaja, am stiut ca sunt norocos. Ce nu stiam totusi e cat de norocos urmeaza sa fiu. Ce nu stiam e cat de frumos urma sa crestem amandoi, cat de mult urma sa tinem unul la altul si mai ales cat de minunata esti tu. Ma bucur mult ca Grecia a fost doar inceputul pentru noi, nu o simpla amintire care sa ramana in mini-jurnalul tau, si ma bucur pentru fiecare moment pe care il petrecem impreuna, mai ales ziua ta de nastere micuto (*bine, sincer trebuie sa fac niste research, nu stiu pana la ce varsta am voie sa-ti zic micuta*).

De asemenea, imi place mult mult ca ne completam, ca desi nu suntem capabili sa luam decizii independent, cumva amandoi reusim sa facem unele care se termina bine mai mereu. Gen eu decid sa mergem la mare, tu esti fericita ca vedem Urlatoarea si urci surprinzator de bine (*chiar si cand exista sansa sa fi mutat aia cascada*). Eu iti propun sa vii cu mine la munte cu prietenii, iar tu nu doar ca vii, dar esti si minunata acolo pe deasupra (*poate prea minunata, serios ca trb sa fim mai naspa unu cu altu cand iesim in grup:)*)), chiar si sub forma de burrito (*sa nu mai spun ca te pricepi si la fugit de ursi*). Amandoi decidem sa mai stam putin de tot pe plaja, iar apoi amandoi alergam dupa tren. Dar hei, am mancat clatite si pana la urma am reusit sa-l prindem. Mereu reusim.

Toate astea nu sunt doar amintiri aventuroase si minunate, dar si dovada ca orice facem impreuna iese super pana la urma. Si vom mai face multeee lucruri impreuna! Impreuna o sa ramanem cuplul cel mai dragut chiar si fara aniversare din cauza caruia se cearta alte cupluri, impreuna o sa ne dam in continuare pupici d-aia mici asa cum stim noi, impreuna vom avea in continuare cele mai frumoase intalniri tematice (*chiar daca tema este sa stam imbratisati pe banca sau sa mancam pizza 'uitandu-ne' pe Netflix*), si eventual impreuna vom avea si casuta noastra in care sa stam amandoi.

Am incredere in noi, si mai ales in tine, ca vom reusi toate astea. Pana atunci insa, astazi este ziua ta, si la modul cel mai simplu vreau sa iti doresc sanatate iubito, pentru ca dragostea o ai pe deplin de la mine, iar norocul ni-l facem noi amandoi.

Inca o data, iti urez la multi ani, Biut. Nu cred ca am mentionat in astea doua pagini, dar te iubesc mult. Foarte mult.

Dedication

This book is dedicated to all the people who said at least once
"Is this all there is?"
while looking back at their lives.

P.S. – It is not.

Table Of Contents

- Introduction -

I want you to look around. Look at the people you see and tell me what similarities you notice. If you aren't in a public place then think at the people you know and observe things they all have in common. I will take a shot in the dark and guess some of these things. Let's see: middle class? Trapped in a routine? Having 9 to 5 jobs or even multiple shifts? Overall happy with their lives but still having that "I could do better" feeling?

Do not tell me if I got any of them right, just reflect on your answers. I should probably start by making it clear that there is nothing wrong with being in the middle class or having a regular job. This is how most honest people live their lives and this is how our society works. What is wrong is to settle on this and stop trying to improve yourself. What is wrong is knowing that your life could be better and still refusing to do anything about it or simply procrastinating until it is "too late". Even though it has become a cliché, keep in mind that **"the chains of habit are too light to be felt until they are too heavy to be broken"**. It is unclear who said that first – starting with Samuel Johnson in 1748 and ending with Warren Buffet in our days – but whoever said it was certainly a brilliant mind considering the truth of this statement.

You see, the simple fact that you are reading this introduction is telling me two things:
1) You probably aren't where you want in life right now.
2) You are ready to do something about it, which is a very good beginning.

Before starting, I want you to know that your journey to become an expert negotiator and thus getting the most out of your life will not be a short nor easy one, so you have to decide right now if you really want to make some major improvements for yourself. If the answer is negative, you can stop right here.

-

-

- Ok.

Are you still with me? Good. I am going to show you how **this book will solve problems** that you do not even know you have and how it will help YOU **get the most out of YOUR life.**

As a reader, you deserve some kind of assurance that this is worth your time, and the best one that I can give you is this: please. I am begging you to become a better version of yourself, and I guarantee this will be among the most useful 2-3 hours you ever spent doing something.

While analyzing everything I learned over the years, I realized that 90% of life comes down to one thing: **negotiation**[1]. Most of the information I was receiving was teaching me, indirectly, one way or another, how to negotiate.

After quite a long time of constantly using and sharpening this skill, I started to see how much power it actually holds and I felt the need to include everything I knew about it in a more compact form. This is how this book was born. If you ask me now, the reason of writing was rather egoistic as I didn't intend to publish or even write a book. All I wanted was to get all my knowledge about this essential skill in one place so I will never forget any detail, but as I was writing I decided that more people should have the chance to **learn something that is so important without spending years on reading books and thousands of hours watching different videos related to this topic or talking with hard-to-reach people.**

In less than 100 pages you will not only learn how to better understand other people and get the best outcome for every situation, but also how to better evaluate yourself, your priorities and the things around you. You will develop side abilities besides the main one discussed – negotiation – that will increase your capabilities in many different areas and thus improving your whole life. Remember that this book is based on studies and experiments which have their origins in the real world, so I am practically offering you the results of years of both theoretical and empirical studies which aim to help you understand and get the best out of every real life activity.

I promise that if you read and follow through every little thing that I wrote here, your life will change radically (in a good way). Like all the great things in life, it will not happen overnight or in 2-3 weeks, but if you are consistent and you do it the right way (based on what you will learn here), you will inevitably become more successful and **you will start to get the most out of your life.**

This is something we all should have learned since we were young, but that does not mean it is too late to do it now. There is a powerful Chinese proverb which says: "The best time to plant a tree is twenty years ago. The second best time is now.". You will never get a better moment than this one to start living the way you want, so my advice for you is to not miss it. If you do, you may regret it in less than twenty years. I will be waiting for you at the end of the book to clarify a couple of things and to share some good news. Also, here is a little spoiler: if you like riddles, you should really get to the end of it. See you there!

Chapter 1
- What does it actually mean? -

In life everything comes with a price, and it is our duty to negotiate it in our favor. And no, we are not talking only about money, we are talking about everything. Whether it is the price for that car you dream about or choosing the next holiday destination with your family, all the things that you want can and have to be negotiated.

The interesting yet often ignored thing about negotiation is that it's absolutely everywhere. We are used to automatically think at money when we hear this word, but the truth is that it actually surrounds us in every aspect of our lives. Remember when you were a kid and had those 30 minutes talks with your mother about why she should let you stay up on TV until 10:30 PM instead of 10 ? Or when you were in school and you had to convince your teacher to not give you homework over the weekend? Or maybe that time when you managed to make all your friends agree to your decision regarding a trip? Those were all negotiations, whether you realized it or not.

One of the unwritten laws governing the economy is that individuals always have their best interest in mind when it comes to decisions. People never do something without asking for another thing in return. Despite this being true and demonstrated, there will always be people who will argue that "I only want the best for X" or "I don't want anything in exchange, I do it because I'm a good man". This is complete bull&#!t, but it does not necessarily mean they are lying because many times this happens we are not aware of it. Nobody gives anything for free, there is always something that is expected in return. What most people misunderstand is that "something" can mean anything from money, services, a simple smile or just a sense of fulfillment for themselves.

Once you understand and accept that people, including yourself, do not do anything for free, you have an edge over the competition. That edge comes from the simple fact that if you are aware of this thing you will stop doing it unconsciously and start taking advantage of it like you should.

That being said, just because you ask or offer something to somebody it does not mean you negotiate, right? Negotiation represents an advanced way of asking and offering things and while it may look easy I can assure you it is not that simple. The basic "can you lower your price a little?" may be easy, yes, but negotiation has much more to offer than just that. People know and use elementary mathematics and physics daily and it looks easy, but we did not build the ISS using only basic algebra skills. Learning the foundation in every domain is not a big deal, but if you want to achieve great things you need advanced knowledge in that specific field. The more knowledge you possess, the bigger the things you can accomplish.

If you read through the definitions of "negotiation" you will find, depending on the source, different forms that basically have the same meaning. In the Cambridge Dictionary it is written that negotiation is "the process of discussing something with someone in order to reach an agreement with them, or the discussions themselves". I also ran across definitions like "method by which people settle differences, the process by which compromise or agreement is reached while avoiding argument and dispute" or simply " interpersonal decision-making process". While all of these are true, in my opinion none of them is complete or at least generally applicable. Each one of them is correct, yes, but every definition that I found is simply too objective and academic to properly explain such a social-related word. I can understand that a definition – especially the one you find in dictionaries – is meant to be as objective as possible, but if we really want to understand words like "negotiation" we must shed a more subjective light on them. From my point of view, negotiation is represented by **any act – physical or mental – that has the purpose of obtaining the best possible outcome for a situation.** If you accept that definition – my definition – then you will quickly realise that you already negotiate more than you thought.

It may sound a little bit too selfish, but if you pierce through the layers you will see that it is actually true. And why wouldn't it be? It is natural for every individual to seek the best for himself, so it would be foolish to judge such behaviour. This does not mean you should start screwing people over in order to get the best for yourself just because "it is natural". Remember that "the best outcome" does not always have material references. Know your priorities!

Ok, so we already spent some – too many – lines only to briefly explain what negotiation actually is. I promised to myself that I will keep the information in this book as concentrated as possible (you will discover later why), so let's jump to "why should you spend your time reading this book and master that skill even though you just found out that you are already negotiating and it has gone pretty well so far". I will give you two short clues:

1) You have a lot more to find out.
2) You will miss out on many things if you don't.

14

Chapter 2
- Why should you do it? -

If you think about it, we already answered – indirectly though – this question earlier, when we talked about how I define negotiation. We agreed that it has the purpose of obtaining the best outcome possible, and I never heard anyone saying "nah man, I do not want the best for myself, I want bad things to happen in my life".

While this reason alone should be enough to get you motivated, it is not the only one. It may be the most important one, yes, but there are others that you should consider as well. The first thing that you should have in mind when thinking about why you should negotiate is the simple fact that **you can.** Negotiation is a skill, and like any other skill, it can be learned and practiced by anyone.

So *why* should you master this skill?

1) It is probably the most important thing that they do not teach you in school!

Remember when you were sitting down at school and had that 8-hours day where you were learning about which is the capital of Nigeria or the calculus of second derivatives? If you remember that, then you probably also remember asking yourself "when will I ever need that in real life" without ever getting a proper response. You know why? Because there isn't one. Most of the stuff you learned in school is – almost – useless (compared to the stuff they do not teach) but I will not go into that as this is not the subject of our book. The point is that when you encounter life, you realize that even though you know what is the atomic mass of aluminium and that mitochondria is the powerhouse of the cell, you do not know how to socialize properly, how taxes and money work, how to make something by yourself and certainly not a single thing about NEGOTIATION, the main skill that can help you get the most things in life.

I am a firm believer in the fact that every human should have a strong foundation of general knowledge before choosing a certain domain to master. However, in my opinion, the education system today (and implicitly all the people who are a part of it) has gone a little bit too far with this "foundation", up to the point where it became a whole skyscraper with not enough room and time left to discover the things that people actually want and have to learn. This leaves them with a long list of things they are supposed to understand by themselves and that is not an easy thing to do. The problem appears when you have to examine your options in order to start somewhere but you don't know where, so let me give you my advice: the first and one of the most important things you should learn is how to negotiate properly as it will prove to be a very useful skill that will help you learn the others with ease.

2) It is one of the most universal skills that you can possess!

The funny thing about life is that no matter how you live it you will eventually end up hitting your head on a ton of different situations that will require different competencies. The things you try to avoid the most? Sooner or later you will most likely have to do them as well. I like to believe that this is the reason why schools are feeding us with such a wide variety of subjects in our first 4-5 years of learning. Yes, I know they do that for 12 years or even more, but 5 years is what I find acceptable so let's stick with that.

As you put more candles on your birthday cake, you can observe that the situations you encounter are becoming more and more complicated. Life goes from "what color do I want my bicycle" to "where should I work" or "how and where do I buy a house" really quickly, so you have to be ready for anything, but being ready for so many things is impossible. I mean, even changing a lightbulb requires a certain amount of knowledge and you only do it once every few months, but you still know how to do it. You also probably know how to change a tire, even though you did not have a flat one in years. These are skills that you do not require regularly, but you still possess them either because you needed them at some point in life or you think you will. The problem is there are only so many things that we can know how to do, so it would be very useful to learn some more general ones that you can use in daily situations. We are talking about skills like talking, driving, cooking and of course, **negotiating.**

You may not drive every day, or you may not drive at all. You can go a few days without cooking too, but as we said at the beginning of our book, one thing you will most likely be surrounded by wherever you go is negotiation. It has been like that since life began on Earth (life, not humans) and it will be like that until the end of it. I guarantee that after you learn this skill, the only thing you will have in mind will be "why didn't anyone tell me these things before?".

3) Negotiation gives you a sense of fulfillment!

Did you ever feel proud of something you made all alone, when nobody supported or even knew about it? I am talking about that something you have put your time and tears into and in the end you realized it was all worth it. You probably did, so you know this is one of the best feelings possible. That sense of fulfillment and self-appreciation you have when you just finished the whole thing, you take a short break and just say to yourself: "I DID IT!". It is a feeling nonpareil. This is the exact feeling you get every time you finish a successful negotiation.

Constant negotiation brings you an unrivaled sense of appraisement as long as you do it right and you get to discover a lot of unknown things about yourself and your abilities. An important part of mastering the skill of negotiation is constantly practicing the things that make you worthwhile. Successful people are those who know their value but do not overestimate themselves, so be cautious not to become arrogant while you are at it.

4) You meet new people and develop new abilities!

We are again talking about something you can not read in a book or watch online. Something that is not taught in schools or learned from your parents. We are talking about the things that you can only learn by constantly doing them until you get good and comfortable. These days, basic things like meeting and talking with people became a real challenge for many of us. Doing these two things **the right way** is even more complicated, but if you want to achieve great things in life you have to master them and the only way to do that is by repeating it on a regular basis. All the books that you read about "public speaking" or "how to approach people" are totally useless without practice. Even this book will be almost useless without practice, but luckily for us negotiation is something that you practice daily, so you might as well learn to do it well. A mentor of mine used to say that one of the best ways to constantly become a better version of yourself is to do something that makes you uncomfortable every single day. Talk to that person, go to that place, jump from that airplane! Ok, maybe not the last one, but you get the point.

Remember that stepping out of your comfort zone and trying new stuff is the best way to grow and this is exactly what negotiation does, among other things. You will see that every one of them is a unique experience with new characters from which you can learn something and with whom you can create new friendships. Experiences are the fuel that adjusts and improves not only the skill of negotiation but also your speaking abilities and many others. The more experiences you will have, the more prepared you will be for life.

5) You will eventually learn the true value of things!

You may know how much a phone or a car is worth. This is simple, you look in the catalog. You can also know how much a pencil, a book or an ice cream costs by going to the nearest shop. But how about things that you cannot find brand new with a price tag already attached to them? How can you appreciate the price of a course, a service that you need or anything that you do not find in stores? The answer is simple: negotiation. Only by negotiating enough and mastering this skill you will eventually learn to put a price – be that money or something else – on things that have no fixed value.

I hope that the reasons I mentioned made you understand both the power of negotiation and the need to master this skill in a world where everybody tries to sell you something.

To give you a quick example of what negotiation can do, I will tell you a little joke that I heard a few days ago :

"Two workers were doing their daily jobs at the manufactory. One of them was called John and the other Blunt. John notices that Blunt was smoking while working, which was not allowed inside the building. A bit angry, John asks Blunt:

John: Why are you allowed to smoke? I asked the boss if I can do that and he said I have to wait until the lunch break.

Blunt: This is funny, I did not have that problem. How did you ask him?

John: I asked him if I can smoke while working and he refused immediately!

Blunt: See? This is the difference. Instead of asking that, I asked him if I can work while I smoke a cigarette and he agreed without saying anything else."

I want you to read that joke again and see how a slightly different expression can drastically change the result of a discussion. This is just one little example of a haggle tactic, and you are about to learn even more – some of them much more powerful – tactics like that. Before we talk about what to do when the negotiation already started, you should first learn how to properly prepare for it.

Chapter 3
- How to prepare for a negotiation -

Sooner or later in life, after stumbling across all kinds of problems, there is one rule that most people learn: never dive head first into a problem which you didn't encounter before, or you may make it worse.

Negotiation is no exception to this rule because every one of them is different, and when you add the fact that a big part of its outcome is a result of how well each person prepared for it then you quickly realise how important this step really is. There is no cheating when it comes to it, so you better come with the lesson learned.

To properly prepare for a negotiation there are a few boxes that you must check on your little to-do list:

1. Make sure you know what you want

Before anything else, in every negotiation you have to know what you want to obtain. You must decide for yourself the minimum and the maximum you can or want to get from it. That way you will know where to start the negotiation and how to coordinate it in your favor. Also, you can make a little imaginary exercise in which you are the other person – the one you are bargaining with – and see things from his/her point of view. If you do that, you are much more likely to know what replies and remarks to expect and thus you'll be prepared for anything. (e.g., when you were very young and ready to ask your mom if you can sleep over at your friend but before asking you were thinking at all the ways she could say "no" so you could prepare a comeback).

Setting your expectations is crucial for a negotiation and if you do it right it will run much more smoothly for you. Remember that negotiation doesn't necessarily have to be a stressing act, at least not for you.

2. Gather information

If you want to have the upper hand in a negotiation, you have to collect information about both the person you are negotiating with and the object of negotiation. This is relatively easy to do because nowadays we have that thing called "internet" where you are one click away from any information about anything and – in some cases – anyone. Doing this will not only give you a huge advantage in the negotiation but will also help you avoid making a bad transaction or being tricked. As an example, if you want to buy a car and the only thing you know about them is that they run on fuel, they must have a steering wheel and you want it to be red – women are usually in this situation – then someone can easily sell you one that "has sit in the garage of an old lady for the past 10 years" at a high price, and little you may know that if you would have brought a mechanic he could have told you that you are about to buy a rally car which had 2 accidents in the last couple months. This is why you always have to know more than a thing or two about the object of negotiation.

When it comes to the opponent, it may be a bit harder to gather information but that doesn't mean it is impossible. After all, you don't have to know the place where he was born or his first pet's name. A quick research about his knowledge/experience in the field should be enough. Also, it is recommended to search some precedent negotiations he has made or talk to people he did business with in the past so you ensure that you also want to do business with that specific person. Try to understand what he wants to get from you and how much he is willing to bargain so you know what strategy to adopt and what tactics to use.

3. Build your strategy

Now that you decided what you want to get from the negotiation and you gathered all the information you could about the object and the other party, it is time to analyze everything you know and create your strategy. At this point you want to have at least an idea about every question that may be addressed to you while negotiating and even more important than that, you should have in mind all the things YOU want to ask. This is a little secret that not many people know and I want you to write it down: **whoever asks the questions controls the conversation.**

I will say it again: whoever asks the questions, controls the conversation. This is very important. You do not want to be the one that does the most thinking. Instead you want to be the one that gathers the most information and put the other in a slightly stressful position. What? I said YOU have to be relaxed during the negotiation, not necessarily the other person.

When thinking about your strategy, you have to keep in mind:

- what you want to get (the best/worst case scenario)

- the first offer (even though most of the time it is better not to make the first offer)

- the type of negotiation (to decide whether you should do it alone or bring someone, talk in person or on the phone etc...)

- who is your opponent (his background, what he wants from you and how bad he wants it)

- how bad you want the negotiation object (whether it is money, services or other things)

- what negotiation tactic(s) would work the best.

If you are a more emotional person then you may also consider to carefully pick a certain place for negotiation (somewhere you feel comfortable) and practicing in front of the mirror. Also, if you are a relation-oriented type of person, you can ask your "opponent" to meet up a few times before actually doing business. The most well-known people for doing this are the Japanese, who will always meet at least a few times and befriend whoever they want to do business with. Also, the Japanese businessmen are some of the finest negotiators on Earth, but it may be just a coincidence.

On the other hand, if you are business-oriented then you want to avoid any relations as this may affect the way you negotiate and how you make decisions.

Always keep in mind that a negotiation begins well before the actual meeting so you want your preparation and your strategy to be flawless.

Chapter 4
- Negotiation techniques -

Negotiation is an art and its subtilities are countless. There is no such thing as "THE strategy" or "THE technique" when it comes to it because every situation is different. Because of this, if a strategy you used in a negotiation had success that does not mean it will help you in another, therefore you must be able to improvise, adapt and overcome.

Many people have tried to find the secret formula that would win every negotiation but no one succeeded. Fortunately for us though, even if they haven't found THE way – a way which probably doesn't even exist – they discovered many useful tactics that will certainly help you win a lot more bargains than you would without them.

We are talking about techniques that helped the wealthiest people in the world create their empires and that can help YOU become a master negotiator.

Even though I would like to talk about all the techniques I know, I will try to keep it short for the sake of the book – and the sake of your time – and only expose some of the most powerful and useful ones, as follows:

1) The exaggerated offer technique

This tactic is often used when you are not sure where to start the negotiation and you want to have what I like to call "maneuvering space" – the possibility to make concessions without affecting what you wanted to obtain initially. It consists of launching a slightly bigger (or smaller, if you want to buy) first offer than the price you want to get and the price your opponent is probably expecting.

When you apply this technique, there are two things that can happen:

A: You will eventually go as low (or high) as you initially wanted to obtain so it's good anyway.

B: You will walk away with a much better deal than you hoped.

You have to be careful though because if you overexaggerate you may ruin the negotiation. Do not insult the other person with your offer.

To help you better understand this tactic, I will give you an example of where and how you can use it.

Let's say you want to sell a computer that you do not use anymore and you mark it as "negotiable" on an advertisements website. A potential buyer[3] calls you and asks how much you want for it. You know that your computer is worth around $300 and that is a fair price for it, but you also know that if you start the negotiation at $300 there is no way you will get that much. Also, you are not sure how much the buyer is willing to pay. In that case, instead of asking directly how much you want ($300), you exaggerate a bit and say "I'm thinking at around $400", and then – optional – continue by explaining why you ask that price (it wasn't used very much, it has big storage memory, it belonged to and old lady in Germany, whatever you think it's worth mentioning). You know your potential buyer is interested in what you are selling – otherwise he wouldn't have called – so he will probably begin to haggle by offering you $300 or even more. At that point, you can either accept it or keep bargaining for a better price. The important thing is that you already obtained your desired price – almost – without even negotiating, just by using this technique.

2) The kamikaze technique

I wasn't able to find a proper name for this one in specialty literature so I came up with one myself.

The kamikaze technique is used by experimented negotiators to gain an initial advantage over the opponent. It implies launching, besides the main offer, a secondary one that is not that necessary and is a bit exaggerated. Even though you know very well you do not really need the thing you requested in the second part, your opponent won't know that, and more importantly, you know he will not agree with it. Since it is unlikely to refuse both your offers, he will most probably choose to accept your main request and – sometimes – even be grateful that you gave up on the second one.

To better understand this technique, I will give you a real-life example where you can use it.

Let's say you want to go to a theatre with your partner but you know he doesn't have enough time. Also, you know very well that he hates shopping and he would do almost everything to avoid it. What you can do to make sure he will accept to go to the theatre is applying the kamikaze technique with "shopping" as the spare option.

The conversation would sound like this:

You: "You know, sweetheart, I was wondering... do you have some free time this weekend? I was thinking that we could go shopping and maybe to the theatre after."

Him: "I have a lot of work to do this weekend and I certainly don't feel like shopping. Can't we just go to theatre instead?"

(You did it! You already convinced him to do what you initially wanted. Now you just have to "play the victim")

You: "Ok... I guess the theatre is good enough."

Him: "Thank you!"

(See how it works? Not only you obtained what you wanted, but you also made him be grateful for the deal he THINKS he made so you do not owe him anything!)

This technique is very powerful and the best part about it is that you can use it in countless situations. You can literally use this in 99%

of the negotiations you make and it is proved to give you the upper hand in most cases. Anyway, keep in mind that this is an advanced technique and you will need some exercise and skill before you can pull it off perfectly.

3) The "Triple-yes" technique

The "Triple-yes" technique is more of a psychological trick that is proved to work due to what is called "deductive reasoning", a characteristic possessed by most rational beings.

The key is to make your opponent say a successive number of "yes" (usually three) to what appears to be random and unrelated questions before advancing your offer.

One of the best examples that can show the applicability of this technique is something we all encountered: the charities.

If you have ever been addressed at your doorstep or somewhere on the street by fundraisers from different charities, you certainly had one of the two possible dialogues. The first one (the amateur and also the most used one) is the basic "Hello sir, I am from organisation X and we are raising money for Y". This is a straight forward way of saying it, but it is not so efficient because it gives you plenty of ways to refuse. The second kind of dialogue though, the one used by experts, would sound like this:

Them: "Hello sir, do you have a couple minutes to talk?"

(now, even if you know that these words never bring something good, you probably say "yes" out of respect)

You: "Yes."

Them: "Do you consider yourself a good person?"

You: "Yes."

Them: "And do you think a good person helps people in need?"

You: "This is true, yes."

Them: "Indeed it is. You know, the reason we are going door to door is that we are raising funds for a charity which helps kids born prematurely. Can you help by donating even a little bit?"

You (as a good man that you already said you are): "Yes...let me bring my wallet."

See how easy that works? They did nothing but ask you questions that seemed totally random until they made sure you can't go back from your answers so you had to do what they initially wanted.

This technique requires a little bit of speech preparation as you have to assure they will answer "yes" to your first 3-4 questions and that their answers will indubitable influence their final decision. However, if you manage to get the speech right, there is almost impossible to mess up, so you got yourself a deal.

4) The first offer technique

I know, I know, "Arthur, didn't you say that I should not make the first offer?". Indeed I said that, but this is not what this technique is about. It is more of an exception, a "what to do if..." .

One of the most frequently asked questions when it comes to negotiation is: "Should I make the first offer?". The answer (with some exceptions) is still NO. You should not make the first offer, because by letting the opponent do it you can take a pretty accurate guess about what he has in mind and also establish what I call the "**negotiation range**". This term refers to the minimum and maximum of a negotiation, including all the values between.

But what do you do when the opponent doesn't want to make the first offer? In that case you will have to do it – "and it's easy, we use the exaggerated offer technique,right?". Well... not always.

When it comes to this, you should know that your first offer should not be an extreme one, simply because sometimes you do not know what "extreme" means. In most cases, when you are selling something with a fixed value on the market, you can start the negotiation using the "exaggerated offer technique", but in special cases when even you aren't sure about how much the thing you are selling is worth, you should always let the other person make the first offer and try to adjust afterwards. Considering this, generally you will have to set the negotiation range.

The reason why this range is so important is that it gives you crucial information about your opponent's future offers.

Let's say you want to sell a house that is worth $130 000, your desired price would be $150 000 and your lowest price would be $100 000. If your buyer offers you $110 000, then you already have your **subjective** negotiation range: it sits between $110 000 (your opponent's first offer) and $150 000 (your desired price). But this is not the only information you can extract from it. Now you can also take a guess of what your opponent's negotiation range (the **objective** negotiation range) looks like. If his first offer was $115 000, then you know that this is HIS desired price, and you can also guess that his intended price (the one that he actually thinks he is going to pay) is probably around $125 000 while his maximum would probably be near $140 000. Now that you know that, you know how to proceed with the negotiation in order to obtain his highest price.

This range itself is not too effective if you use it alone, but when you combine it with other techniques it becomes one of the most basic yet powerful tools a negotiator can have and it will give you the ability to never make a bad deal or waste precious time.

Why does it save time?

Simple. If the opponent's first TWO offers are too low, then you might as well walk away. I'm saying the first two because some people will initiate the negotiation with a small offer in an attempt to look "aggresive", but they usually correct it in the second offer.

5) The false offer technique

This is a technique that some people would call "unethical", but I chose to include it in our list for two reasons:
- it is extremely effective
- it is widely used

So what is it about? Well, the false offer technique is something that affects both the seller[2] and the other buyers. In fact, the only person that wins something out of it is YOU.

This tactic has the purpose of eliminating the competition (i.e. the other buyers) by making an offer that is high enough to not be surpassed by anyone. That way, most of them – actually all of them in general – will give up and walk away. After this happens, you retract your original offer and the negotiation has to start all over again, but this time the only potential buyer it's you, so it becomes much easier to obtain a good deal.

You have to consider that this technique cannot be used everywhere because in some cases you will have to pay immediately so you do not have the possibility to retract your offer. Also, in some places it might even be illegal to do that, so make sure you know what you are doing.

The best scenarios where you can apply it are the auctions (even better if they are online) and the negotiations in which the payment is made over time or at least a few hours/days after the deal is made.

Most of you probably already figured out how this works, but I will give you an example to make sure everyone understands what I'm talking about.

Let's say you are watching an online auction for a pair of limited edition J's that you want to buy and that you cannot find in stores anymore. The auction just started so the price is still pretty low, but there are a couple of hours left of it and there are many people willing to bid. What you can do in this situation is to advance the false offer technique. If you do that, the auction would look like this:

Person X: *bids $75*

Person Y: *bids $100*

Person Z: *bids $125*

(when you think the price has raised to how much you would be willing to pay, make your move)

You: *bids $400*

Person X,Y,Z: "Who the #@!% is this guy?"

Person X,Y,Z: *abandons the auction*
(After that happens – and most of the time it does – all you have to do is wait until the auction is 10 seconds away from ending with you as its winner, retract your bid and make the seller an offer of what the last bid was – in this case, the person Z with $125. You have a high chance to make the deal if the price was fair enough.)

Before using this technique make sure it is legal to retract your offer so you do not get caught in your own trap. Use it with caution and only when it is totally needed.

6) The rapport technique

Pretty much like the "Triple-yes" technique, this one is more of a psychological trick, but it operates in a totally different way.   This time it is not about WHAT you say but rather HOW you say it.

This technique is based on the proven fact that people are more likely to listen and agree with those that act and think like them. I will not talk about psychology and why that works here, instead I will show you how to actually use it.

It implies creating a rapport – hence the name – between you and your opponent and use it to your advantage. In essence, the rapport refers to the speed, the voice and the tone your opponent uses.

So when negotiating with someone you have to keep in mind the following rules:

- if your interlocutor speaks with a high tone, then you must use a high tone as well
- if your interlocutor speaks with a low tone, you must also lower your tone
- if your interlocutor speaks fast, then you have to speed up your speech too
- if your interlocutor speaks slowly, then you should slow down a little
- if your interlocutor takes pauses between words, you   should   also do   that
- if your interlocutor emphasizes a certain part of the phrase (the verbs / the pronouns / the nouns) on a regular basis then you should do the same.

These are the most important things you should pay attention to in a conversation. It is true that you can observe many other things but assuming you are a beginner in the art of negotiation this is more than enough.

It may be hard at first to keep track of all these little things but with the time it will get easier so you should not give up if you can't do it right on your first attempt. You must practice until you will master this technique because you can use this with almost everyone and it gets amazing results every time you do it.

Also, you must learn to do all of these without making it look like you are mocking the opponent, because nobody likes that.

7) The "good cop-bad cop" technique

Movies. This is what you must have in mind, because this tactic appears in countless movies. I've seen them, you have seen them, everyone has seen them.

We are talking about those movies where two cops arrest one guy and desperately try to make him confess his crimes. In most of these movies there is a pattern: they use the "good cop-bad cop" technique, inspired by the real-life method used by police.

So how does it work? You probably already guessed it: it consists of two people with contrary temperaments. One of them is always the "good guy", the one that is trying to help you and to get you the best deal there is, and the other one is the "bad guy" who usually threatens you in order to obtain what he wants. The purpose of this technique is to make you think you made a good deal (by listening to the "good" guy's advice) while in reality you just did what the pair wanted from the beginning. I am using the word "pair" because the "good cop" and the "bad cop" always know each other and their scripts are made and learned well before the negotiation has started.

It usually has the same scenario: the good cop enters the room and starts telling you about how bad the situation is and how he could help you get the best out of it. Also, he always mentions the other cop, the "bad" one, who is determined to turn your life into a nightmare. A few moments later, the bad cop joins the conversation and takes his tough and unyielding position. When he is done, the good cop starts playing the role of the moderator in your conversation with the bad cop and in the end he makes you accept his offer.

Even if most people are aware of this technique, it always gets good results because people get easily intimidated.

One of the best occasions where you can use this technique is when you buy something second-hand.

Let's suppose you want to buy a car. You already saw it online and now you have to meet with the seller and check it out. The best thing you can do before meeting is talking to a car mechanic (ideally a friend of yours) and bring him too at the meeting. In this case, you will be playing the "good cop", while your friend will be the "bad cop". So when you arrive at the meeting with the seller, the dialogue could look like this:

You: "So this is the car you want to sell, right?"

The seller: "Yep, this is it."

You: "I will be honest with you, the car looks really good to me, but I do not know much about cars so I brought a friend of mine who is a car mechanic. He will check it out and tell me if it's all right. After that we can talk about the price."

The seller (already a bit anxious): "Of course, check it out! This car is as good as new!"

(You start looking at the car, the interior and the design elements. The mechanic turns it on, revs the engine, check the wheels and all the other moving parts that can present problems)

The seller: "So? What do you think?"

The mechanic (talking to you): "I think you shouldn't hurry. There is a reason why this man wants to sell it. This car has seen better days!"

The seller (visibly annoyed): "What do you mean?!"

You: "Relax, it cannot be that bad, I really like this car. How much do you want for it, sir?"

The seller (discouraged, he wanted to start the negotiation at $9.000, but now he changed his plan): "I would accept $8.500 for it."

You (talking to the mechanic): "What do you think? Is it worth $8.500?"

The mechanic: "Right now, I don't think it does. $8 500 is how much you would have paid if you had bought it two or three years ago. Personally, I wouldn't pay more than $7.000 on it."

You: "Come on, it has to be worth more than that! The interior is very clean and the exterior also looks nice. Sir, can you drop the price a little bit? I am ready to pay you $7.250 right now!"

The seller: "The car is worth more than that! Give me at least

$8 000."

You: "I would sir, but the mechanic said I shouldn't even pay $7.000 for it. Can we agree on $7.500?"

The seller: "All right... I think I can do $7.500."

I think you figured out how the "good cop-bad cop" technique works. While it doesn't require much skill, you must have a good synergy with your partner and a well-made script before the negotiation starts.

8) The black or white technique

This is a very effective technique that experimented negotiators use when they have multiple options which work for them. It has the purpose of making the other person think in your terms and always go with one of your options.

When asking for something, most people do it in a way that gives the other person the possibility to choose from a wide range of options (even if some of them are not desired) and this is something a professional negotiator does not want to happen. These are some examples of questions you want to avoid:

- "Where should we go on holiday?"

- "What color do you prefer it?"

- "Where do you want to eat?"

- "When do you want to meet?"

I want you to pay attention to the wording of these phrases. Notice anything similar? They all have in common one thing: they give the other person the possibility to choose whatever they want, even if not all the answers are good for you.

So what can you do the change that? The answer is – duuh – the black or white technique. The way it works is by making your opponent think in your terms, asking questions that contain your favorable options. By doing that, you are forcing the opponent to choose the best option out of those you gave him and not think about the other possibilities. So, instead of asking questions like those presented above, you can ask them like this:

- "Do you want to go to Greece or Spain for the holiday?"

- "What color do you prefer it, green or blue?"

- "Do you want to eat at KFC or McDonald's?"

- "Do you want to meet at 5 or at 7?"

See how a little change in the wording of a phrase obliges the other person to choose an answer that is favorable to you? They think you give them the opportunity to choose what they want, when in fact you are only giving them options convenient for yourself. Remember what Blaise Pascal said in his "Pensées" masterpiece: "Words differently arranged have a different meaning, and meanings differently arranged have different effects".

Anyway, this technique has its limitations and it doesn't always work properly. For example, when asking a "black or white" type of question, the interlocutor may say "turquoise". Or even worse, he might say that he doesn't want anything at all because he is undecided. Even when that happens, this technique may still be useful by helping him decide what he wants.

I advise you to practice and use that technique as it is not a complicated one, it is not aggressive at all and most importantly it is extremely effective. To be honest, this is one of my favorite techniques to use in day to day life. Don't want to go to a romantic movie with your girlfriend? Ask her if she would rather see a thriller or an action one. Can't go out with the boys on Thursday? Ask them what they would prefer between Sunday and Friday. This technique can get you out of so many situations...it's simply amazing!

9) The two-requests technique

This technique was studied a few decades ago and it is scientifically proven to work even in our days. It works by firstly requesting something easy to accomplish and then advancing the main request.

The first request is launched with the purpose of creating a contact with the interlocutor. Once he accepts that first request, experiments show that he is much more likely to accomplish the second request as well.

This works because once the interlocutor was kind the first time, it is much easier for him to be kind again. I will give you a short example to help you understand this technique.

Let's say you have to complete some surveys by asking random people on the street (I am sure we all encountered this at some point). If you go to someone directly and ask if he has a couple of minutes to complete your survey, you will probably get a quick "sorry I don't have time". What you can do instead is go to someone and ask them if they know where you can get some good pizza – because who doesn't love pizza – and let them explain to you. After they are done, just before leaving, you can say something like "thank you... also, can you give me 2 more minutes to complete a short survey? I would really appreciate it". They are much more likely to accept now that you created a contact and they already helped you with something. If you think the pizza example is a bit too random don't worry, there are literally hundreds of ways you can approach someone with a little small talk, you just have to be creative. Or search on the internet. Both methods work just fine.

Even though it may seem easy at first, you have to be careful when using this technique because there are some things you have to keep in mind. The first thing you have to do right is deciding your first request. You don't want a request that is too easy to accomplish because you might not create a contact strong enough, but at the same time you do not want a request that is too complicated because it will give the interlocutor the feeling that "they have done enough". Another thing that you have to consider is the time between the requests. While in some cases the second request can be advanced only a few seconds after the first one (like the example above), in other cases you have to give a window of a few hours or even days before you ask again.

There is a variety of real-life applications for this technique but you always want to adapt it to the context and to the interlocutor in order to get the best results.

10) The "it can be done" technique

This technique is as simple as it is efficient. It basically means adding a premise to your question that requires a positive response. There is a list of questions (premises) that a negotiator has to know in order to perfectly master this technique and take 100% advantage of it, but I will only teach you the one that – in my opinion – is the most important: "**HOW EASY WOULD IT BE TO...**".

I want you to write down these words: "how easy would it be to". I know it sounds trivial but trust me, these words are magical.

To help you understand how to actually use this technique I will tell you a personal story.

Some time ago I was heading home from a short trip to the beach side and as a very punctual person that I am, I managed to miss the train by a few minutes. Bonus – the next train heading home was scheduled in like 8 hours. So right now it's like 11 A.M. and I have to spend almost a whole day in this small town. This means 8 hours of enjoying the sun and to walk alongside the beach, just wonderful, right? Actually yes, if it wasn't for the luggage. For a single person, I had a lot of luggage with me and considering that I wasn't planning to sleep in the train station the whole day I had to do something with it. Realizing this, I did what any rational being would do – go back to the hotel where I slept the nights before and ask them to store it there for the day, but of course it wasn't going to be that easy. After I arrived back at the hotel, I was welcomed with a warm "sorry but we don't have room for any luggage and if you leave it here we are not responsible if anything happens to it". However, the receptionist who told me this was also a human, so it was worth a shot: "Look, I understand that you don't usually do this, but how easy would it be for you to put these bags somewhere safe only for a few hours?". The answer he gave me was exactly what I hoped: "not very easy". Why was I hoping to get this response? Because it basically meant it was possible, and possible it was. After a little more chit-chat he showed me a little storage room where I was allowed to keep my luggage safe in exchange, of course, for a small price. Seven hours later, I came back and it was all good, then I headed to the train station where – finally – I took the train home.

Other situations in which this technique helped me a lot and it can also help you include: avoiding fines, extending deadlines, convincing people to do certain things, etc...

11) The Columbo technique

I want you to remember this ground rule: **whoever asks the questions controls the conversation.** You should already know that since I mentioned it a few pages ago, but I will probably keep repeating it because it is essential.

As a rule of thumb, you should be doing approximately 20% of the conversation, while your opponent does the other 80%.

I mentioned this again because the Columbo technique is based on that rule. It represents your main tool in a negotiation when you do not have enough information and you want to find out more about something – the object of negotiation, the opponent or others – without asking directly.

The purpose of this tactic is to obtain information that you do not possess, and for that you will have to "play the dummy". You may look a little bit foolish while you do it, but this is exactly what you want. You have to count on their vanity, which is not hard since the number one quality of most people isn't exactly the humbleness.

Try to be curious, even when it comes to things that you already know. Instead of saying "Yes, I am aware of that" say "Oh really? Interesting, tell me more". You will be surprised by the amount of information you get without even specifically asking for it. Another notable advantage is that you are not only getting extra information, but you are also verifying the credibility of your negotiation partner, and that thing is crucial.

This is not a hard technique at all since the only thing you have to know is that "you don't know". Even more, it can be modified to get certain information that you may be interested in.

Let's suppose you want to know if someone drives a blue car (I know, dumb example, but it proves the point). One way you can find out is by picking a random blue object and start talking about YOUR blue car that has the same shade (it doesn't really matter if you own or not a blue car). The conversation could look like this:

You: "This is a nice pen. You know, I used to have a car exactly the same color. It was a Dodge Charger."

Him: "Hey, I had a Chevrolet that was the same color!"

You: "Have you? Well, mine was a special one, it was from the limited '68 edition."

Him: "Well mine was a '69. Convertible!"

You: "There aren't too many of those around."

Him: "Yeah, I got it from a guy down on 26th Street."

See how it works? Vanity and over-sharing, things that most people show often. He gave you 3 extra details without you even asking for them. But it can still be better. Do you see what's wrong with the dialogue above? You simply **TALKED TOO MUCH.** Remember that 80-20 rule from the beginning? It is still available.

I want you to close the book now and write a new dialogue where you only contribute with around 20% to the conversation and still get the same amount of information. You can even change it if you want because I am pretty sure you will never care if someone drives a blue car nor will you want to compliment a pen, but this works the same way in lots of situations. The only thing you have to do is practice and learn to adapt it, depending on what you want to find out. After you are done, open the book again because you have much more cool stuff to learn.

You may also want to use Columbo's trademark line, which is ″**...just one more thing**″ – add that followed by something you want to know right before leaving when the person has relaxed (thinking that the ″interrogation″ is over) and you will have a much bigger chance to get the information. If you need help with this line go watch the series online, trust me, it is worth it. After all, nobody can teach this better than Columbo himself.

Before jumping to the next technique, I think this is a good occasion to tell you the three magic words which I learned from one of my mentors and I believe every seller should know. Are you ready?

I DON'T KNOW. Did you expect that? I don't know if you did, but this is the best answer you can use when trying to sell something.

These are probably the most powerful words you can use in sales. I know this sounds shocking because as sellers we are supposed to have all the answers, right? Yes. But what happens is, when you know all the answers, you lose control. So instead of hurrying to answer all the questions, try to slow down a little. Take a look at some examples:

- "Is your product any good?" – I don't know... depends on how you define "good".

- "Will this help me?" – I don't know... what do you exactly need help with? Tell me more about your situation sir.

- "Are you honest with me?" – I don't know, what do you mean by "honest"?

- "Why is your product so expensive?" – I don't know sir, why do you think people pay me so much money?

Always answer a question with a question. Stop explaining everything. Remember, **whoever asks the questions controls the conversation.**

12) The projection technique

This is the kind of technique that you will want to use in dead-end situations where it seems like you just can't "win" the negotiation. You probably observed it in some movies as it is pretty popular among the salesmen societies.

The only thing you need for mastering this technique is some creativity and background information about the other person beliefs, because you will be projecting your conversation (at least for a short period) in another space and time that is going to shift your opponent imagination like a bunch of 'shrooms.

Follow these dialogues:

- A: " Why are you dressed so sporty, this is a business meeting, I can't take you seriously!"

- B: "You know, the biggest deals were made on the golf course."

(you just changed the space to a golf course which would justify your outfit and also induced the idea of a big deal)

- A: "Are you cheating on me? You didn't answer your phone the whole day!"

- B: "By that logic every time someone's phone dies he must be cheating."

- A: "I don't think I should invest in this, it is too expensive."

- B: "Over five years you will be so rich that you will start to laugh just by thinking that you almost refused this offer."

(you made him think about his future, which is "guaranteed" to be a bright one if he accepts your offer)

Notice how making some out-of-nowhere assumptions we can drastically change the idea of a phrase? There are many ways you can use this technique, the only thing limiting you being – as I said in the beginning – your own imagination.

There are many varieties of this tactic, one of them being "the absurd proposition". It is pretty much the same but it goes a step forward, so it can either be a lot more effective or totally useless, depending on the situation. Sometimes when an argument gets too complex and confusing, people find it easier to just accept it rather than keep trying to win.

13) The "cheap things are expensive" technique

How do you sell something that is expensive? The answer is **value.** You have to make people understand the value of what you are selling. The hard part is figuring out what does "value" mean for your potential buyer.

From experience I can tell you that the price isn't the only thing people look at when they buy something. Here is a short list containing a few more "valuable" attributes that I noticed people are interested in:

- who is the seller (his reputation, his attitude, the brand itself etc...)

- immediate benefits

- long term benefits

- testimonials (the opinions of other people)

- presentation (how you exhibit the object/service)

The key is accentuating the advantages your buyer finds valuable. Let's say you want to sell a car that is in good condition and thus it has a bigger price tag. If a potential buyer tells you that "he has seen cheaper", one thing you can do is a little wordplay. For instance, if you notice your buyer is interested in immediate benefits, you may ask "what exactly was cheaper, the car or the repairs that you will have to make a few days after you buy it?". Or if he seems like a long-term thinker, you may say: "Yes, you could probably save yourself a few hundred dollars if you buy a cheaper one, but before doing that you should consider that one day you could be left on the sidewalk or even worse while driving to your family reunion because you decided to save money today."

Another way you can make him understand the value of what YOU are selling is indirectly telling him. You can use phrases like "I am ok with people selling cheaper than me, every person knows the value of what he is selling".

There are many ways to adjust the questions for this technique depending on the situation and the buyer, but I think you see the point. It's all about making your potential buyer think in terms of value, not numbers.

14) The emotion technique

Before we can talk about this tactic, I want you to write down another rule: **people buy because of emotion, not because of logic.**

I know this may sound wrong but believe me here. Every time people buy something, they buy it because of emotion and justify it with logic. They are buying feelings.

I want you to think about something that you want to buy and ask yourself "why do I want to buy that particular item". I mean it, close the book for a little bit and ask yourself that thing.

If you pierce through the layers, you will see that what you actually want to buy it's a feeling, an emotion. Your car, your house, your pet, every major thing that you ever bought was more than just something you physically needed – it was an emotion.

Think about a real estate agent. What is he actually selling? I can tell you for sure that he is not selling a house. A house means a kitchen, a bathroom and some bedrooms. No, he is selling more than that- he is selling a **home.** He is selling the place where the buyer's kids will live, the place where he and his spouse will grow old in, the place where his friends will come over. This is what he is actually selling. He is selling emotions.

If you manage to understand this whole emotion thing, you won't only master negotiations, you will master your whole life. I personally first heard about it from one of my mentors – yes, another millionaire – and I can tell you it changed my life in a positive way. Learning how to appeal to your buyer's emotions instead of his logic is probably the most important thing that you can ever learn in negotiation.

To give you an example of what it can do, I will tell you what happened to someone I know. He was in a suit store browsing a piece for some event that he was invited at and a staff member asked if he could help him with anything. The conversation went like this:

Staff member: Can I help you with anything?

Him: I'm just looking, thank you.

Staff Member: Sir, can you do me a favor and try this costume?

(He didn't want to be disrespectful so he put on the costume.)

Staff Member: How do you feel, sir?

Him: Well, I feel pretty good.

Staff member: Do you like James Bond movies, sir?

(He was like "duuh, who doesn't ?")

Him: Of course I do!

Staff Member: "Well sir, you should know that this is the same suit design that James Bond wore in the "Casino Royale" movie.

What do you think happened next? Before you know it the guy bought the suit. He didn't buy it because of logic, there were plenty of other costumes that looked good there, he did it because of how it made him feel.

Read that dialogue again and understand the power that emotions have on someone's decisions. After that, take a short break to think at all the things you want to buy and reflect on why do you actually want them.

15) The disregard technique

How do you differentiate the good negotiators from the bad ones? This is a question I got asked and also asked myself many times before. At first, even I wasn't sure about the answer because there were so many things to considerate, but after giving it a second thought I decided that the most important difference is that **"the amateur sells, a master makes people want to buy."**!

We all start as amateurs, but it is our duty to become masters. Making people want to buy is not an easy task, but it definitely can be done. One part of achieving this skill is learning how to appeal to the buyer's emotion (this is the reason why this technique is number 15 and the emotion technique was number 14).

Another important part is making your buyer understand that **he needs you**, not the other way around. Of course, you do not want to be arrogant or anything like that, but you do want to induce the idea of **scarcity.** You want your buyer to feel lucky for doing business with you.

After presenting your offer, this is what your buyer should have in mind:

- You are not selling anything, you are helping him solve a problem.

- You do not lack of clients.

- You do not make business with everyone.

- You care about what he wants to achieve.

If you do it right, by the end of the conversation **you** should be viewed as the **buyer** while your opponent becomes the **seller.**

I personally fell victim to this technique some time ago when I bought some custom-made furniture for my house. I went to the best guy I knew in the business and told him about what I wanted. After that, I expected a logical question like how soon do I need my furniture to be done or details about how I want it to look, but he did not ask any of that. Instead, he started to smoothly ask things about my personal life, like where do I work, how old am I, why do I want to change the furniture and so on. After I answered all those unexpected questions, he said: "Do you know why I asked you those things?". Of course I had no idea, so I told him I don't. His response shocked me: "Because I do not make furniture for everyone. I want to make sure that you deserve what I have to offer". Indeed, I knew he was the best, but even if I didn't, he would have convinced me with that line. He basically told me that he does not sell to anyone. Same principles as Rolls-Royce and other major brands use for selecting their customers.

He then continued to tell me about some other potential clients that he refused simply because he did not like them. How do you think

I felt after hearing this? Privileged would be the best answer. Even lucky I'd say. He perfectly reversed the roles and made me want to buy his services.

It is true that this technique will not work with anyone, but you have to think about it like that: who would you rather buy from – a salesman that is desperately trying to sell you something or one that knows the value of what he is offering and does not try to convince you? I think we both know the answer.

16) The hypnosis technique

Also called the "dual-voice method", this technique originates from the Ericksonian Hypnosis which was invented by Milton H. Erickson, a famous psychiatrist of the 20th century that used to treat some of his patients by "seeding ideas" in their subconscious mind.

How *ethical* it is to use that on people is still up for debate, but if you decide to use it you have to know how to do it correctly.

Practically speaking, to master this technique you would need probably a few years of training and a degree in psychiatry, but when using it in negotiation you don't actually have to be an expert.

I will not go into all the subtilities of this technique as this book wouldn't be enough to talk about all of them, but instead I will break it down for you and make it as simple as possible.

The main thing that you have to learn is this: **when addressing to the subconscious of a person you have to speak in a lower voice/tone than usual.**

The next logical question would be "when should I lower my voice during the conversation". Well, the best moments when you could use it are the ones when you talk about some key-aspects, like the biggest advantages that your product has, or when you want to induce emotion-based ideas (safety, pleasure, satisfaction etc...). It is proven that suddenly lowering your voice during a conversation instantly gets the interlocutor's attention and make him more interested in what you are saying. Also, experiments show that lowering your voice usually makes the other person lower his/her voice as well, so do not be scared if that happens.

I personally don't use that technique too often, but I have a friend that does use it frequently and gets amazing results with it. He is working – or at least he was the last time I saw him using it, now I heard he got promoted – as a door-to-door salesman for a skincare company and one time I had the opportunity to see him in action. He was presenting some kind of body lotion to a woman, talking about what it does to her skin while testing it on her hand. I could not help but notice how every now and then while talking about basic things about the lotion he would suddenly lower his voice and almost whispering key things like "see how good it feels on your skin" or "you won't believe how soft your skin will be in a few weeks" and then going back to his normal voice and talk again about basic stuff. After a few times doing this he almost convinced me to buy it too, even though I didn't even try it. All I could think about was how good that lotion felt on the skin and the amazing results it will have in a few weeks.

The good part about this technique is that you do not need a partner to exercise it. You can simply take a random text and try to speak it out loud while lowering your voice at the parts that you find important. Feel free to practice it as much as you want.

17) The "no more" technique

Most negotiations are nothing more than a series of concessions and this is something we all know. It usually follows the same steps: the seller names a price, the buyer asks a lower one then the seller drops it a little bit and then the buyer offers a little more and so on and so forth until they meet somewhere in the middle. Of course, this is valid only for amateur-level negotiations, which represent roughly 90% of all negotiations (yes, I just came up with that number but it probably isn't far from reality). When talking about professionals, this rule will not apply anymore, since at high levels negotiation is more like a game of chess.

The question is: what happens when you are in one of those 90% and you reach that middle price but you realize that you do not want to pay – or accept if you are the seller – that much for it? Well, since you can't really say "actually you know what? I am taking my last offer back" in the middle of a negotiation, one thing you can do is a little math in your head to calculate how much "the middle price" will be, depending on his first offer and your first offer.

This will indeed help you to be ready for the disappointment, but won't really change the course of negotiation since the concessions will be the same, right? For example, if you want to buy something and the seller asks $1000 then you may start the negotiation by offering $700. After that, the seller would probably make his first concession and ask $900 instead of the initial $1000. Now you are obliged to make a concession as well, so you would probably offer $800. When this happens, you already know that $850 (or $800 if you are lucky) will be the price you will have to pay because there are no more concessions to make on your side - you reached the **middle price.** Of course, you could have calculated this price since the seller made the first concession, but that wouldn't have helped at all. So the question remains: what do you do when the middle price isn't convenient?

In situations where this happens, the best thing you can do is to use the "no more" technique.

This technique is all about sending a message without actually saying it. You want your opponent to understand that you already offered too much and you are not willing to negotiate any further. In order to do this, when you decide that there are no more concessions to be made and the final price won't be the one you wanted, you should make one more offer: the one that is most convenient for you.

To help you understand how to apply it, I will take the example above again but this time we will use the "no-more" technique. When we do that, the conversation will look like this:

You: "How much do you ask for this?"

The seller: "I can sell it to you for $1 000."

You: "This is way too much. I'm offering $700."

The seller: "I cannot accept that price. How about $900?"

You: "It is still a little exaggerated. I can give you $800."

The seller: "Let's meet in the middle. I am willing to sell it to you for $850. This is my best price."
(at that point you realize that there are no more concessions to make and you do not want to pay even $800, leave aside $850, but you still want the item, so you apply the "no-more" technique)

You: "Well, I am willing to give you my best price as well: $750."

The seller: *speechless*
(after a short pause of perplexity, some sellers will agree to sell the item for $750 or maximum $800, which is your last biggest offer in this case. If they refuse, at least you don't have to pay more than you want)

Using this technique, we didn't only obtain the desired price, but we also made the seller give us a better price than his "best price" by leaving him with only two options: end the negotiation or agree with OUR price. Even more than that, we did this in a way more elegant manner than the classic "nah I can't accept that, I'm going home".

Like any other technique though, this one is not guaranteed to work every time. Most of the negotiators will react as the one in the example above, but some of them won't. Even if that happens, it is worth learning it as it can get you out of many unpleasant situations, but I still recommend you do not use this one if you are negotiating for something you really want and can't get from somewhere else.

18) The personality technique

Each one of us has a different personality and you have to remember this every time you talk to a new person.

In every conversation, the faster you realize which are the key features of the interlocutor's personality, the better you will be able to empathize with them and create a stronger bond between you two.

The problem appears when you realize that what we call "personality" can – and most often it does – have a lot of "key-features". Like... a lot. Keeping track of all of them may be hard – if not impossible –, but fortunately for us we do not have to do that. In fact, there are only a few of them that are worth observing.

This is more of a tool than a tactic itself because you can use it in association with any other technique. Even more than that, it can also be used when you are not negotiating for something because it helps you decide how to talk with each person depending on his or her type in order to have a pleasant ordinary conversation.

Below you will see the most important personality patterns on which you can group people and thus decide how to interact with them.

Proactive / Reactive

"Does the person want to take the initiative or prefer to let someone else do it?" – this is the question answered by this pattern. Before learning how to talk to each type, you have to learn how to identify them.

Proactive people initiate. They have a tendency to think little to less about consequences and get into different situations without properly analyzing them. They may seem arrogant and sometimes even annoying because of this "obsession" of doing things their own way and not listening to others' opinions. They are the kind of people that will START and FINISH a task, no questions asked, and they almost never wait for someone else to take the lead.

Reactive people, on the other hand, are pretty much the opposite. They are calm and analytical regarding even the little problems and most of the time they wait for someone else to take the initiative. They often think and analyze a problem without ever taking action. Believing in faith and luck is a good indicator for this pattern as most reactive people tend to do so. Also, they never start a task without completely analyzing how to do it and taking into consideration all the bad things that may happen. They are the people with whom you want to talk if you want to make sure that a task will be done well.

Since there is no fixed question to ask in order to find out if a person is proactive or reactive, you have to pay attention to other things like how they **talk** and how they **move.**

When talking, a **proactive** person tends to:

- do it very fast

- use short phrases

- do it like they are in total control of the situation

- be direct about what he/she wants to transmit

As for the movement part, you may observe things like:

- gesturing a lot

- be eager and impatient

- being unable to sit down for long periods of time.

A **reactive** person on the other hand will most likely:

- use long and incomplete phrases (no subject or verb)

- use many infinitives and conditionals

- talk like the other people are judging him

- talk about thinking, analyzing, understanding or waiting when it comes to almost everything

- sit down for as long as they can and avoid to move their bodies.

Knowing what type of person someone is can prove to be a very important thing as it allows you to use the proper language of influence.

When you want to convince a proactive person to do something, you have to use sentences like: "do it", "don't think about it", "why should you wait", "take the lead", "you can do it", "right now", "best time is now", "you will miss out".

However, if the person you are talking to is a reactive one, it is more appropriate to use: "let's think about it", "we should analyze this better", "you have to completely understand that", "you will have good luck", "it might [...]" etc..

Some people can be both reactive and proactive and in that case it is ok to use both languages of influence depending on the situation, so do not worry if you can't tell for sure what type of person someone is.

I am getting close to / I am getting away from

The question this pattern answers is "What motivates a person to take action?". Just like the last time, we will first learn how to identify them and after that we will talk about the language of influence.

People with the "I am getting close to" pattern have their eyes on the prize. They only think about their goal and are very motivated to achieve it. They are very good at setting priorities and are always very enthusiastic when it comes to accomplishing tasks that get them closer to their objective, but focusing too much on the target often makes them ignore possible obstacles and that can lead others to think they are naive.

The "I am getting away from" pattern belongs to the people who are focused on the present and are trying to solve current problems. They are very good at identifying issues and discovering possible obstacles that may appear along the way. Setting goals can prove to be a difficult task for them and they can be easily distracted by minor problems. Also, they are strongly impelled by deadlines.

Recognizing each pattern is easy as people tend to have very specific traits.

The "**I am getting close to**" people will do things like:

- talk about winning, taking, having etc...

- mention his goals and generally what he wants

- point to things when talking about them.

- use proper language: "I want a solution", "I want results", "The risk is necessary" etc...

The "**I am getting away from**" people will:

- talk about current problems and what should be avoided

- only think for the short-term period

- complain about situations that have not yet happened

- gesture only when they want to emphasize something negative

- use specific expressions like: "I got a problem", "I had enough of...", "I want to avoid...", "I don't want to risk" etc...

(Note – listen to what a person says after using "because" as it will usually be an indicator for his pattern and always use "why" in your questions)

Let's use the context of moving to a new city in order to visualize the differences between the two patterns:

You: "Why do you want to move to a new city?"
I am getting close to: "Because I will meet new people and exploit new opportunities."
I am getting away from: "Because I will no longer have these loud neighbors and I will break the routine of my daily life."

The **language of influence** for **"I am getting close to"** people is: "to obtain", "to get something", "to possess", "it will allow you to", "the benefits/advantages are...", "you will have" etc...

When talking to **"I am getting away from"** kind of people you should use phrases like: "you won't have to", "you will escape from", "avoid", "there won't be problems", "you will get rid of" etc...

Options / Procedures

"How does one think?" is the final question that we will address in our list. To answer it, we will use the Options/Procedures pattern which is a simple one.

People with an "Options" type are the inventive ones. They always try to find new and better ways to solve common problems and they find it difficult to follow those that already exist. Changing and breaking rules is their specialty and they are engaged by new projects and opportunities. They often avoid – and even dislike – making decisions and are easily distracted.

On the other hand, the "Procedures" people tend to follow instructions and avoid trying new things. Once they start a task they have to finish it no matter what. They are interested in **how** to do things, not **why** we do things that way.

Just like we said above, in order to identify what type of person you are dealing with, you should use "why" in every one of your questions.

When doing that, a "Procedures" person will most likely answer to "how", not to "why", thus ending up telling you a whole story.

Example:

You: "Why did you choose this car?"

PP: "Well my last car broke down and I had to replace it real quick so I called my cousin who knows a guy that sells cars and he put me in contact with him and asked me what car I want so I told him to give me one that won't break in the next couple months because I need it for work so he gave me this one." *breathes*

An "Options" person, however, will always give you a list of criteria and the other options that he has/had.

Example:

You: "Why did you choose this car?"

OP: "I wanted a reliable car that has a strong engine and that was convertible. Also, I wanted it to be German so I had to choose between X,Y,Z. In the end I chose X because it looked better than the others."

When you are trying to convince an "Options" type of person you want to talk about:

- the opportunities he will have

- the choices he has

- "I am willing to bend the rules for you"

- a better/new way to do things

If you are talking to a "Procedures" one, you should use expressions like:

- the correct way

- these are the steps: first, we... then... in the end...

- it is verified

- it has worked before

There are many other aspects to talk about here, but these are the main lessons that you need for now. There are many books out there that you can read if you want to deepen your knowledge regarding this subject and I strongly advise you do to so.

19) The scarcity/deadline technique

Time is a key element in negotiations and if you are skilled enough it can represent a big advantage for you. At the same time though, if you do not know how to use it, it will play against you and it will become a massive drawback.

One big mistake that most amateur negotiators – sellers in general – make is giving people too much time to think after presenting their offer. Think about all the things that can happen when you give people too much time to make a decision:

- they may find another seller to buy from

- they have time to think your offer in logical terms and that usually reduces your chance of selling because they may realize it is not necessary to buy (remember – people buy because of **emotion**)

- they may delay the buying process to the point where they no longer need the item or service.

This is why you have to create the feeling of **URGENCY**. Get a piece of paper right now and write that word down. This feeling can be created two ways: establishing a limit of STOCK for your offer, or a limit of TIME. Since a limit of stock usually has the same effect on people (it makes them want to buy **faster**), we will only talk about the limit of time.

The simple act of setting a **time limit** or a **deadline** to your offer can get amazing results, and this is why it is so widely used. And yes, even though you may not observe it every time, it is used very, VERY often by professional sellers. This is actually one of its biggest advantages – once you master it you can do it so gracefully that people will not even notice.

Let me give you some quick examples of situations in which this technique was applied on you and you probably didn't even realize. Have you ever seen an online or offline offer that sounded like "Buy this item in the next 6 hours and you get 1 FREE / 50% DISCOUNT / PICKLES SUPPLY FOR LIFE" ? You probably did. They are most often used in teleshopping but you can observe them in many offers at any store, even online. Another variation of this technique is the "ONLY 4 MORE IN STOCK! HURRY UP BEFORE THEY ARE GONE!" which creates an urgency of stock and implicitly of time. And what happens most of the time when you see an offer like that? You may either buy it or not, but one thing that happens most of the time is this: you open the TV/laptop the next day and you see the same offer that has supposedly ended yesterday, with the same time limit / stock. And you do this again the following day and see the same thing, and then again and again and so on until you realize that the "6 hours" deadline turned into "6 days" or even more. I can tell you that I've been personally seeing this TV commercial for some cooking pots on teleshopping with the same "BUY IT **TODAY** AND YOU GET ONE FREE!" for 4 YEARS. That's right, four years. And counting. Do I feel stupid? Yes, because I actually bought that item the first time I saw the commercial, so it worked on me. More recently, I fell for something like this again when I bought an online course (on a well-known platform) that was "90% off only that day". Guess what – that course is still "90% off" as I am writing this.

I am not saying you should do that, because it could harm your reputation – after all, it is a pretty dirty trick – but what I am saying is that it is a very efficient method that you can use without drawing any attention if you do it right.

Do you know who else is very good at using this technique? A kid. If you do have a child – or a younger brother/sister – you probably noticed it. Kids are somehow born as highly skilled negotiators but they lose that ability as they grow. For example, let me tell you what my little brother did when he was about 7 years old. My dad was driving him to school one day and all the little guy talked about the whole road was how much he dislikes math and the homework his teacher gave him. When they arrived in front of the school though, my dad couldn't find a parking spot so he had to turn on the hazard lights and stop on the road until my brother would leave the car. At that moment, when the people behind him were already getting angry, while stepping out of the car, my brother said: "Ohh, I forgot to tell you! My teacher is organizing a trip to the chocolate factory and it only costs $70. This is the last day we can pay! Can I go, please? I will explain more tonight". What was my dad supposed to say? He rushed to give him the money so he could leave faster since there was already a line formed behind him and my brother was running late. This is the same kid that a few days ago was selling nuts for $0.5 a piece and after getting enough money he started selling chewing gum.

This only demonstrates that the deadline/scarcity technique can be used with success even by a kid. I only gave you a few examples, but there are countless ways you can use it. I advise you to not abuse it, though, as it can lead people to think that you are not serious.

20) The link technique

This is a technique that you want to use in most long term negotiations, when you have to build a relationship with the "opponent" in order to develop mutual trust and find the best deal for both of you.

It is scientifically based on how we as humans are hardwired. You see, our brains have a tendency to create **links** between certain memories and certain feelings. This happens involuntarily and once it is done it cannot be undone, at least for a long period of time or until a stronger link replaces it.

I am talking about things like:

- that time you ate something new that made you feel sick and now every time someone mentions that food you have a repulsion feeling

- that time you almost died from drinking too much of a certain alcohol and now you almost throw up when you only smell it

- that perfume which automatically makes you think about someone you loved

- that time when you visited a new place and you took a souvenir so now every time you look at it you remember the good time you had there

- that 3rd-grade notebook or that old collection of stickers you found after a few years in the attic that instantly made you think about your childhood.

There are many other examples like these. The point is that once your brain creates a link between a certain thing and a feeling or a memory, it is very hard to break that link. This is why you should try your best to only create links with **good** feelings.

The same principle can apply in negotiations, where you often have to develop a relation with your "opponent" before proceeding to business. There is a long way between making a transaction with someone and making a genuine business partner. Whether it is about business, future or current relationships or simple friendships, if you want to build something stable that will consist as a source of happiness in the long run, you will have to use the link technique.

Just like the examples above, the main thing you want to do is create links in the mind of your – potential – partner in such a way that his brain will associate **your image** with a good memory or feeling. In business, this good feeling usually represents a good deal that he had with you or an opportunity that you gave him. But what do you do when you just started and you haven't made any business yet? In this situation, that "good transaction" memory can be replaced with another – maybe a bit more friendly – one. I selected a few things that are proven to create strong links and that are generally available to use, but you can complete that list depending on your partner's character and your preferences.

1) Select a unique place for meetings

People get excited and they remember things that they see for the first time in their lives. This is why we enjoy so much to travel and we remember every place we visit in foreign countries.

When picking a place for a meeting with your partner, you do not want it to be a common one. I can guarantee that nobody gets too excited when they hear about another meeting in a regular restaurant or in some park alley they visited hundreds of times. This is why you want to pick a more uncommon and beautiful place that you think they have not visited yet so they will attach that pleasant memory to your image. It does not have to be somewhere expensive or far away from where you live. It can be that part of the town that looks stunning at the night, that top of a building with an amazing view or even that public garden full of flowers. Anything you think is impressive will do, as long as you do not forget to keep in mind your partner's character and personal traits. For example, you do not want to invite someone who is afraid of heights on top of a building or someone who is allergic to flowers in a garden. You have to know who you are dealing with.

(Note- as you probably already thought, this can be used in way more situations than "business" related ones)

2) Don't keep it all business

A business meeting does not have to be only about business, especially when you are seeing the other person for the first time and you intend to develop a long-term partnership with him. It is true that "business" will be the main subject of the conversation, but it should not be limited to that. If you want to create a good impression you will have to do more than the usual talk.

People are fond of smart people and you want to be seen as one. There are two main ways to do that: you can either be very good at what you talk about (in this case business), or you can slide some unrelated interesting things into the conversation that will make the other person think about you after the meeting is finished. Since – in my opinion – one can never be "too good" at business, I suggest you use the second option.

I remember when I attended some kind of conference where a few select and smart people had to give us a speech on a specific topic. I liked each and every one of them, but one particularly impressed me. He didn't really have the best speech and he wasn't necessarily the smartest, but what he did perfectly was delicately changing the speech subject every now and then and talk about astronomy. Apparently he was very good at astronomy, so he used that to his advantage, even though the speech topic had nothing to do with it. He was doing it so gracefully that people did not even realise at the moment, projecting the whole room into the abyss of the Universe with incredible metaphors while sticking to the subject. I think I wasn't the only one impressed by him as he received thundering applause from everyone. He is also the only speaker whose name I still remember and I think that really means something.

If you are highly knowledgeable in a particular field, don't hesitate to subtly lead the conversation to that subject in order to impress the other person. Also, don't be afraid to crack a joke or two every now and then, but be careful when doing that as people are very easily offended nowadays. Keep in mind that one good line can get you remembered for a lot of time.

3) Tell a stunning story

One of my mentors once told me that every person must have **THAT story**. That story which you tell when someone asks you to tell a story. That story everyone knows about and knows you because of it. That story which everyone would want to hear over and over again. That story which... ok I think you got the point.

It is up to you what **your** story will contain. You decide if it will be about that night you got drunk in a forest and you had to fight seven mosquitos and a bear while figuring out the way out of his cave, or if you want it to be something more elegant with a strong message. As a precaution, you may have more than one so you will be able to pick depending on the context.

I cannot tell you what story to choose or how to narrate it, but I suggest choosing one that you can tell to everybody and that will put you in a good position. Remember, a story can get you remembered very easily. It's up to you if it will be a good memory or a bad one, but the link it will create in people's minds will be very strong.

4) Choose unique activities

Let me ask you a quick question: what do you remember better, the football game you played with your friends last week or that festival you participated at 2 years ago? I do not need an answer from you, I just want you to analyze which one brings more feelings of joy no matter how much time has passed since it happened.

What I'm trying to say is that unique activities are linked to unique feelings that will live in your mind for a lot of time. This is why you have to be very careful when choosing an activity that will include your potential business partner.

Doing this is not always recommended since there is a soft line between **business** and **friendship** that – some people say – it shouldn't be crossed. However, if you think you have a friendly enough relation with your partner then you may consider inviting them to do something together. The "what you can do" in this case is very diversified since it depends on many factors. It can be anything from an art exposition, a movie premiere, a shooting range etc...

Just keep in mind that when doing things together you must have your partner's preferences as a priority, not yours, so be very careful what you pick.

Remember to not bother with this technique if you are only trying to sell your old Xbox to a 15 years old. It is a complex and refined technique that requires time and attention, but it is all worth it if you want to develop healthy long-term partnerships.

Chapter 5
- Talking...but done right -

We said that negotiation is an art, and we all know that in art you do not only need some paint and a good brush to create a masterpiece. If it would be like that everyone would be an artist. Besides the main tools, an artist needs a lot of skill and training.

Your essential tools as a negotiator are the techniques that you previously learned, but they aren't enough if you want to become an "artist". If you want to be an expert, you must learn how to **talk** like one.

Knowing a lot of stuff is not enough in today's world if you do not know how to talk with people and express what you know. In fact, one could argue that it is almost useless.

I cannot say if it's useless or not, but what I can tell you is this: **the ability to talk to people is one of the most important things you can master**, especially as a negotiator. This is why there are so many smart and yet just a few successful people in the world. Most of them lack this basic but essential skill. And I am not talking only about "public speaking" or other things like that where most people THINK they have difficulties. In reality, the vast majority of people have trouble talking in general, but they do not realize it or just simply refuse to accept it. The good news is that, contrary to popular belief, knowing how to talk to people (two, three or an entire audience) is not something you are born with (heard that, "introverts" ?), it is something that you can learn by practicing.

I've read a "shower thought" a few days ago that sounded like: "once you read the dictionary, every other thing you read is just a remix". This is not only pretty funny, but it also contains a lesson that everyone should learn. We all heard many remixes of popular songs, but we only liked a few. The same principle applies to speaking:

people will notice and like only good "remixes" of the dictionary. This means that knowing words isn't enough, you must know how to use and combine them.

It is true that the best way to learn how to talk to people is by actually doing it, but there are a few tips which can make your learning a lot easier. In the next few pages I will show you how to be more persuasive, how to find a common ground with the interlocutor and how to speak while using the techniques we just talked about in order to get the best results out of each and every conversation.

You have to understand that even though two sentences may have the same meaning, sometimes picking the right one can make the difference between the answers you will get. This can either help you or not, depending on which sentence you choose, so you have to learn to do it right. Of course, before even thinking about what words to use and what form of sentence to pick, you have to establish that rapport that we talked about earlier in order to see what kind of person you are dealing with and how he may respond to different utterances. Only after you do that you can decide which words are more suitable to use.

Below you will see a few examples of pair-sentences that have approximately the same meaning but can get completely different results. I will first show you the general "do not do that" form of a sentence/word and then I will reformulate it in order to maximize the chances of getting a better answer. I said "general" because to some people the "wrong form" could actually be the preferred one, but most people will react better to the right form.

(Note: We will abbreviate the "WRONG" form of a sentence or word with **W** and the "RIGHT" one with **R**.)

W: "I want to tell you..." (it sounds like you are confessing something bad)

R: " I want you to know..." (this time it sounds like you actually care about them and want to clarify something)

W: "It is cheap." (it sounds like the quality itself is cheap, not only the price)

R: "It is profitable." (I think you got that one)

W: "You don't understand!" (it makes people feel inferior)

R: "Let me explain again." (shows that you are a reasonable person that is willing to help)

W: "You can contact me." (it looks like you give them the permission to contact you, but you do not really want that to happen)

R: "I am waiting for you to contact me." (here it sounds like you really look forward to talking with them again)

W: "Don't buy from X!" (this one is clearly an order attempt and people don't like orders)

R: "You should buy from us." (while this is more of an advice)

W: "Don't get me wrong." (if you have to say that then it is already too late)

R: "I want you to understand exactly what I am saying." (now that's more like it)

W: "You don't work enough." (it is a reproach that will never make anyone work more, trust me)

R: "You could work more, right? / What would motivate you to work more?" (now it's much more sympathetic and achievable, especially when you also try to find solutions)

W: "Hear me out." (a.k.a. "let me speak while you shut up")

R: " I want you to listen very carefully." (this is much more likely to actually get attention, not only silence)

W: "I can't do it right now." (in that form it is only a refuse without a solution)

R: "I will do it in a few days." (here we got a solution)

W: "Price." (it makes the other focus only on what he is paying, not receiving)

R: "Value/Investition." (it emphasizes what the other person will get)

W: "Offer." (it sounds like he is being sold something)

R: "Benefit." (he has an advantage)

W: "A little." (sounds pessimistic)

R: "More than nothing." (well... more than nothing is better than nothing)

This list can go on forever, but I just wanted you to understand what we are talking about. As a general rule, you must remember that people do not understand the concept of "do not". Not only we do not understand it, but we tend to focus on the exact same thing we are told not to, completely ignoring the negation. When talking to someone, no matter who it is, you must avoid sentences that start with a negation. Instead, try to replace it with a different sentence that has the same meaning but which contains a more positive and reasonable approach.

Also, you want to be very clear about what you want to obtain when talking to someone: you want him to decide, you want him to trust you, you want him to call you and so on. It is preferable to use phrases that demand actions: decide, understand etc...

But what if you want to buy something?

In the previous pages, you observed mostly how a **seller** (as in "the guy who tries to convince others of something", not necessarily selling products) should talk, but in reality there are more buyers than sellers. So how should you talk when you are in the buyer's position?

To be honest, talking is not as important for a buyer as it is for a seller, but it is still part of negotiation so you must master it as well. When someone else is trying to convince you to do/buy something, you should concentrate on other things, the most important one being the "seller". Yes, you must focus on the seller. By that I mean focus on how HE talks, on HIS skill, on HIS approach for the negotiation. That way you can observe if he is trying to use any negotiation techniques or specific language on you, so you will be able to counteract.

Remember that as a buyer you have the upper hand in negotiation. You are the one that has the power to leave without losing anything. The seller, on the other hand, should be under pressure. He knows that if he doesn't make a deal with you he will lose a customer, while you can go anytime to another seller that has the same thing you want to buy, unless the product or service is quite unique. You have to use and maximize this advantage every time you want to buy something.

A negotiation **should not be a pleasant action**. Not for you and especially not for the other person. You have to remain calm and relaxed, yes, but that won't make it necessarily pleasant. **The less emotion you show, the better it is for you.**

To sum it up, you must remember these crucial things:

- whoever asks the questions controls the conversation (see the "Columbo technique")

- you must establish a rapport in order to see who you are dealing with

- you must find and use the proper words/sentences depending on the opponent's personality

- always aim for positive statements and avoid "do not" (negations in general)

- focus more on the opponent's actions and words, not only yours, especially when you are the buyer.

Chapter 6
- More than words: motion -

We already know that talking is an essential skill and the better you are at it, the more success you will have in everything you do. The drawback of this being so important is that you aren't the only one who will try to master it. There are many people out there who are good at talking and this is only making it a lot harder for you to take advantage of this skill.

If you want to have the upper hand against as many people as possible then knowing how to talk is not enough. It is strictly necessary, yes, but is not enough. You have to know how to use more than words, you have to use **motion.** As you probably already guessed, in this chapter we are going to talk about **body language.**

The weird thing about body language is that so many people heard of it yet only a few try to understand how it works. This is because it is a relatively new area that people find difficult to study and explore. Being an expert in body language requires years of practice and a sharp observation skill + a lot of human behaviour knowledge. This is probably why most people are afraid to even try learning it or give up after a short period of time after they started. You do not have to be discouraged though. In fact, this is your biggest advantage. Think about it: if people don't even try it then learning even 1% of what body language is will give you an edge over the vast majority. It may not be easy – at least not as easy as talking – but it can be done. And the results? Stunning.

Taking that extra step in learning the body language after mastering the talking skill and all the other techniques is like obtaining a Ph.D. in negotiation. It is what differentiates the **pro** negotiators, so I strongly advise you to take that Ph.D.!

I mentioned earlier that it takes years to become an expert in the art of *body* language. Also, I mentioned even earlier that we will try to stick to our subject in order to maintain the best utility-per-page ratio[4]. This is the reason why I will only give you some of the main ideas of what body language really is. After that, you are free to deepen your knowledge in this field using other specialty learning materials. I actually advise you to do so as it is a very powerful *skill* that only a few people possess.

Going back to body language, you should first learn what it is and how it works. As a short introduction, body language is a type of nonverbal communication in which physical behavior is used to express – usually involuntarily – information.

People emit information unconsciously through their bodies constantly and this is why paying attention to their movements can tell you more about what they think than paying attention to what they say.

Another big advantage is that not only you will get information, but most of the time you will get **true** information. This is the kind of information that you want to receive, the one that can help you make correct decisions regarding other people and situations. Lying with your lips is easy, but lying with your body is extremely difficult.

If you know biology you can imagine the information you get as a string of RNA that contains both exons and introns. In that case, the true information (the useful one) is represented by the exons, while the other is represented by introns. And we all know what happens to the introns, right...? Wrong, because that lesson was long and we had a math test in the same week. It is ok, I'll tell you – the introns get eliminated, just like you have to eliminate anything that **is not** true information. Ok, I probably lost some of you so we will return to body language. After we are done you can go and read the thing about RNA though, it's interesting, trust me.

There are many parts of the body that you can analyze in order to get this information, but the most important things that you have to observe are:

- The face (facial expression)

- Body posture

- Gestures

- Handshakes

- Breathing.

As I said before, mastering body language requires special training that I cannot provide in this book. However, to give you a better idea of what we are talking about, I will give you some of the most general examples of body language signs and what they represent.

These are the most common actions and postures that you can easily interpret and that will give you the biggest amount of information:

- Eyes looking in the upper right

The direction they are oriented is deceitful because the "right" side, in this case, is an indicator of lie. When someone is looking in the upper right corner while talking they are most probably **making things up.**

In negotiation this is best observed by asking questions. If you are doubtful about the sincerity of your partner then the best way to verify it is to ask questions. If they look in the upper right before answering then they are probably inventing their answers.

- Eyes looking in the upper left

That one is pretty much the exact opposite of the upper right signal. When a person is looking in the upper left side before answering a question then there is a good chance they are honest with you. People usually look in that direction when they want to remember certain things, so you know they are at least trying to tell you the truth.

- Arms crossed over the chest

This example of body language can indicate that a person is being defensive. It can also demonstrate that the individual with crossed arms disagrees with the opinions or actions of other individuals with whom they are communicating.

If your negotiation partner suddenly crosses his arms over the chest then you probably said something he does not agree with or they are simply feeling dominated by you. The best thing you can do in this situation is to simply ask them if they agree with what you just said in order to see where is the problem. Usually, they will tell you what is wrong and you will be able to work it out.

- Pulling of the ear lobe

In negotiation this sign is commonly seen and it is actually a very desired one by the experimented negotiators. People often pull the lobes of their ears when they are tempted to make a decision, but remain indecisive. This movement displays the incapacity of coming to a conclusion.

You want to see this sign because it represents a perfect indicator that you almost made the deal. Usually when that happens the only thing you have to do in order to convince them is adding just a little more pressure by talking about the benefits or the urgency of making that deal with you.

- Stroking the beard or the chin

When one strokes the chin, he or she is communicating deep thought. Such a motion is often used unintentionally when an individual is trying to come to a decision about something. It is similar to pulling the ear lobe, but it is not as good at indicating the temptation to buy. Sometimes adding more pressure when a person strokes their chin/beard will have the opposite outcome, but it is worth a try.

- Touching the nose

This one is a bit more complicated because it can indicate more than one thing. It can be a signal of disbelief or rejection, or it can also demonstrate that an individual is being untruthful about what they are saying.

In negotiation, if people touch their nose while talking there is a big chance that something they said was a lie or at least they are hiding something from you. When that happens you should verify more rigorously what they recently said before proceeding to make the deal.

- Nail-biting

Nail-biting is a type of habit than can demonstrate stress, anxiety or insecurity. It is a movement done unconsciously and this is why people find it difficult to control it.

If your partner is biting his nails during a negotiation then you can consider clearing the atmosphere with a little joke or by changing the subject for a few seconds. Do not exaggerate with this though. Remember, a negotiation is not supposed to be a pleasant experience.

- Head tilted to one side

A tilted head demonstrates that a person is listening carefully and is interested in what is being communicated. A **prolonged** tilted head can also be an indicator of boredom.

This is a very useful signal in the world of negotiation because it indicates which parts of an offer should be emphasized. For example, let's say you are trying to make one of your friends come to a party. You start telling them about where it takes place, the price, the date and when you start talking about who else is coming they suddenly tilt their head. When that happens, you know that this subject – who else is coming to the party – it's the most important one for them. After realizing that, you will talk more about who is coming and make sure you are telling him what he wants to hear regarding that subject, preferably without having to lie. This way you have a much bigger chance to convince him to come to the party and thus win the negotiation. Remember, **a "negotiation" is not limited to money.**

- Standing up straight

This position shows that a person is feeling confident and it is often accompanied by walking at a brisk stride.

If your negotiation partner adopts the "chest up-shoulders back" position it may be a sign that they are very prepared for the negotiation and this can make you feel uncomfortable and inferior. A good option to reposition yourself is asking him a couple of questions that you think he cannot answer or doesn't want to. This should make him feel a little nervous and thus he will probably lose some of that confidence.

We often see this in the political scene, especially during the elections when people tend to argue the most. You certainly saw at least one debate where one candidate is coming with very good arguments and has a well prepared speech about the future of the country or whatever, but everything shatters when the other candidate goes like "You cheated on your 7th grade boyfriend and you expect us to trust you ruling the country?".

See that? No context, no correlation whatsoever with the subject, but guaranteed to break the other person's focus. My example is a little bit forced, of course, but I'm pretty sure you understand what I am talking about.

- Rubbing the eyes

Besides expressing how tired you are, this gesture can also indicate in many cases a feeling of doubt or disbelief for some people.

If you encounter that gesture while presenting your offer in a negotiation it might be a sign that you are losing your credibility over something you just said. What you can do when this happens is to add a question like "Do you agree?". When asked that, most people will tell you what is wrong or what they do not believe, so you will be able to clarify it.

- Tapping or drumming the fingers

Finger-tapping usually demonstrates that a person is growing impatient or tired of waiting. This may happen either because they are in a hurry or they are just bored.

If your opponent starts tapping his fingers during a negotiation then you should try to hurry up a little bit in presenting your offer or just simply jump straight to the conclusion (the price, the benefits, etc...) as he may not be interested in other details. If you just started the negotiation and you see this sign, you should stop insisting on the current subject and go to the next one, repeating this until the opponent changes his position.

- Leaning back / leaning in

Depending on which side the opponent is leaning, you can tell if he is interested or not in what you're saying. When they genuinely care about the conversation, most people tend to lean in to the interlocutor. When they do not care about it, they will usually lean back.

In negotiation, this is a good indicator which helps you decide if you should emphasize a subject or go to the next one.

- Playing "the mirror"

People who are listening closely to what someone else is saying will often unconsciously mirror that person's body language.

You can use this to let people know you really care about what they have to say or you can just observe if the interlocutor is doing it in order to see if they really care about what you are talking about.

- Eye contact

If you don't look the person in front of you in the eyes, he or she may unconsciously assume that you are being dishonest. On the other hand, looking people in the eyes for too long is usually a sign of aggression. To make people feel comfortable and trusted, hold their gaze for just a second or two at a time, but do it often.

Keeping an eye on the interlocutor's eyes is a pretty good option when you want to know if they are honest with you while having a conversation, so it's a good thing to watch out for during a negotiation.

- Palms open, facing upward

An open palm is a sign of openness and honesty. It can be a sign of submission – back in the days when many people carried weapons like swords, this was used to show that they were not holding one – or of sincerity and innocence.

This is a sign that you want to see while talking to someone or especially when you are negotiating because it usually indicates that the person is being honest with you.

These are a few examples of body language signs and gestures that people usually *make*. Learning those signs (and the others if you have the patience) will prove to be very useful in your day-to-day life and especially in negotiations, so once again I advise you to deepen your knowledge in this field. There are many more out there for you to learn, but those that I just presented are the most common ones and the easiest you *can* observe.

You will see that once you decide to learn the body language art, the hardest part will prove to be observing the signals, not interpreting them. However, with time it will become not only easy but a real habit, so keep trying and don't get discouraged if you can't do it on the first try. In the long run it will be worth it.

Chapter 7
- "Subtilities" -

So far you learned why you should negotiate, the techniques to make it easy, how to put them into words and you also took your Ph.D. with the body language lesson. That should be about it, right?

Well... not really, but we are almost there!

Now that we've talked about body language, you should know there are some things even beyond that. They may be considered "subtilities", details that you can totally ignore, but the truth is that sometimes the details make the difference, so it would be foolish to not talk about them.

Firstly I want to talk about **where you should be staying.** Not metaphorical, like... really: where should you position yourself while negotiating?

Most people have a tendency to simply *not* care where and how they position themselves relative to the other person because they think it doesn't really matter. Well, psychology is here to contradict that.

There are not many things to talk about here since we will discuss only the two main places where you have to pick a place.

The first one is, of course, a room. When the negotiation takes place inside a room, the worst position you can choose is sitting in front of the window and with the door behind you. This is because not only you will be distracted by what happens outside, but you will also feel anxious and curious every time the door opens, thus losing your focus. What you should do instead is position yourself in the exact opposite way. If you think about how the furniture is positioned in offices/interview rooms then you quickly understand what I'm talking about.

The second most common place where you are required to sit down is at a good old table. This is something very usual because today most people meet and talk in places where they can also drink or eat something and these places almost always include sitting at a table. When you are in that situation, you should avoid the front-to-front position, because this position usually creates tension and the tendency to argue. What you should be doing is position yourself adjacent to the other person, but not on the same side.

Another thing that many people consider just a "subtility" is the name of the interlocutor. Whether it is the first time you meet or not, you should always remember and **use** your partner's name. This is something that not only makes people feel special but also gets their attention much better than any other way of addressing.

If you have troubles remembering people's names like I do, here is a little trick that will certainly help: every time you meet someone new, after they tell you their name, repeat it two times. It could sound like this:

Stranger: "Hello! My name is Sarak, nice to meet you!"
You: "Sarak...Nice to meet you, Sarak! My name is ..."

See how easy and natural it is? If you do this little trick you will remember names a lot easier than you used to. I dare you to try it the next time you meet a new person.

One more thing you should know when talking with someone, especially if you just met them, is to **never refuse** something they offer to give you.

We have all been there. Like when you had some kind of interview and you've been offered something to drink but you were too stressed out to accept it. Or when you are at a friend's house and they offer you a glass of water or some chips or something like that and you, out of courtesy, probably say "no thanks". Of course, I am talking about a normal friend, not your best friend in whose house you go like it is your own.

This may not seem like such a big deal, but accepting little things that you are being offered can be a game-changer. Not only it is more polite to actually accept it rather than refuse it – and some people may actually feel insulted when refused – but it is also very useful at establishing a relation between you too.

I will give you a personal example. Three weeks ago (and I mean it, what I am about to tell you really happened three weeks ago, at the moment of writing) I was leaving the gym at the same time with a guy that I often observed there but never really talked with. As we were going in the same direction, side by side, only doing a little small talk, he offered to buy me a coffee before taking the bus. Personally, I hate coffee so I had to say no, but I agreed on a hot chocolate. He bought two hot chocolates from a booth (one for me and one for himself) and we kept talking while waiting for my bus to arrive. The first bus arrived pretty quickly but I didn't take it because I felt the need to finish that hot chocolate before leaving (it would have been impolite not to), so I waited for the second. Going from subject to subject, I found out a lot of interesting things about him and I realized that we were alike in many ways. We talked for approximately 20 minutes (until the hot chocolate turned into cold chocolate) and then I had to leave because my second bus came. Since then, though, we became pretty good pals and we talk daily. Even more than that, we plan on doing some business together soon as we have a common interest in something. Remember that it all started with accepting that hot chocolate!

There is a wide variety of situations in which you should remember and use this, all of them having different contexts, but the rule is the same: **never refuse the little things you are being offered.**

One more thing that you should do is avoid checking/answering your phone during a negotiation unless it is something urgent. There are two main reasons why you should do that:

- you lose your focus on the negotiation

- your partner may feel ignored and uncomfortable, reducing your chance of making the deal.

If you are however expecting a phone call that you must answer, then you have to announce it at the beginning of the conversation.

Some people think that receiving phone calls during negotiations makes them look important to the other person so they rush to answer it, but this usually has the opposite effect. Remember: unless i is totally necessary, **don't answer your phone.**

All those little things that we talked about are optional, but I advise you to consider and apply them whenever you have the chance. Remember, there are the little details that make the huge differences.

Chapter 8
- Buying Signals -

Ok, so you did everything: you met with the other person, you established a rapport, you correctly used the suitable negotiation techniques depending on your type of deal, you talked the right way and you observed his/her body language during the whole conversation. Now there is only one more question you have to answer: how can you know for sure **if/when he wants to buy?**

This is almost the last thing that I am going to teach you in this book, but that does not make it any less important than the others. Doing everything right is useless if you cannot realize **the moment when you should press the red button**. The moment when you actually make the deal or not. If you do not press that button at the right time, all your effort could be in vain. To realize when you should do it, you have to learn and recognize **the buying signals**.

These signals will tell you when you should **stop talking / trying to convince them** and actually end the deal. These signals are your red button and you should always pay attention to them. If you don't do it – like many amateur negotiators – you risk ruining even pre-made deals.

Talking about ruining pre-made deals, let me tell you a short story. A few months ago I was in a store looking around and suddenly an item grabbed my attention. I liked it a lot and I was already ready to buy it, but I wanted to ask a question before doing that. I asked the guy who owned the shop my question, he answered it and then he just kept talking. At that point, I was already sold on purchasing the item, but he would not stop telling me about it, about why I should buy it, what other people say about it and so on. I tried to stop him a few times but he was still trying to convince me, even though I was giving him all the signals that "hey, I am ready to buy it, you do not have to talk anymore". But he did not stop. He kept talking up to the point where I left the store because I got annoyed and I also had to be in another place and I was running out of time, so I thought to myself that I will come back to buy that particular item, but in the end I didn't. That guy actually talked me out of the sale. He managed to ruin a pre-made deal, a deal that was made before he even tried to convince me. If *he* would have recognized my buying signals he would have gotten the sale.

You would *think* that situations like this one do not happen too often, but the truth *is* there are a lot of people out there who don't know when to *actually* stop talking.

In order to not be one of those *people*, you must learn a few simple buying signals which will indicate you when to stop trying to con*v*ince people in order to get a deal. The sig*n*als that I selected ar*e*:

1) When the prospect is touching the item.

This is something commonly done by everyone. When we are interested in buying a product, 99% of the time we have a tendency to touch it. When the *p*erson you are trying to sell to is touching and analyzing the item, that is a buying signal. If they would not be interested in what you are selling they would just *l*ook at it from *a* distance. This does not necessarily mean they are ready to buy it right away, but you ca*n* be sure that they are interested in i*t*.

2) When the prospect use possessive statements regarding your item.

This means that the prospect *is* making comments about how life would be like after he buys the item. He is already thinking and picturing himself owning that particular i*t*em. That thought right there is a strong buying signal.

For example, let's say you are selling a car and a guy comes with his wife to check it out. After looking at it, if one of them says something like "this would look very good in our parking lot" then that car is already sold. You do not have to do anything else.

3) When the prospect is asking questions about your product.

Asking specific questions about a product *is* natural when we are interested in buying it. This is done not only because we are curious about what we will own, but also because we want to convince ourselves that we *want* it.

Some possible questions that indicate the desire to buy are:

- "How many do you have ?"

- "Do you have different colors/sizes ?"

- "What materials is it made of ?"

- Etc...

If your prospect asks any of these questions about your item then you should know they are interested to buy it. Questions like these are clear buying signals.

4) When the prospect is asking about the price.

Nobody asks how much something costs if they are not at least interested in purchasing it. However, this question may come in many ways, so you must pay attention. When a prospect wants to know the price of an item, he may ask for it in different ways, such as:

- "How much does it cost?" - this is the most common one and is pretty straight forward.

- "Do you offer any discounts?" - this one is a more subtle way of saying it but it has the same meaning and it expects pretty much the same answer, considering he cannot know the price beforehand.

- "How can I pay for it?" - it means that he is looking for ways to make it work, but is also indirectly asking for the price.

If your potential buyer is asking for the price in any way possible then you got yourself a buying signal.

5) When your prospect is asking about delivery.

Similarly to the possessive statements, when asking about delivery your prospect already made the purchase in his mind and now he is trying to find out when he will get the item. The same thing applies to selling services but the "delivery" may be replaced with "start date". For example, your potential buyer can address you questions like:

- "How long does it take for the item to arrive?"

- "When can we start this?"

- "How soon can we start?"

- "Do you have any fast delivery option?"

If you are asked any of these questions, 90% of the time your prospect is **at least seriously thinking** at buying your item/service.

Those are the main buying signals that are worth mentioning here as they are the most obvious ones. If you focus on those five that I presented you will have a much easier time realizing when to stop talking and proceed to finish the deal.

Even though you may think that you don't need to know the buying signals unless you are the seller, you'd be surprised by their contribution in the buyer's position as well.

Remember, negotiation is not only about money.

Chapter 9
- Do it the right way -

"Knowledge is power. Information is liberating. Education is the premise of progress, in every society, in every family." This is what Kofi Annan, the seventh Secretary-General of the United Nations, once said. I want you to read that statement again.

You can easily observe a big difference between **knowledge** and **education**. Two separate terms that are relative to each other. While knowledge is indeed power, we all know that power is not necessarily good or at least useful if you do not know how to use it. The history and even the present are giving us countless examples of why power is nothing more than a tool that different people use in different ways.

So far everything we talked about in this book had the purpose to give you power. Every "bit of information" that you received can be understood as a unit of power available for you to use in any way you like. But negotiation, and life in general, is more than just power, right?

What really makes a difference is the education, the "premise of progress". Progress starts and derives from education and this is why it is so important to have a good one before anything else. Take example from lottery winners, the people who get one of the biggest "jumps" possible in life. They are given a huge amount of power – in this case the power is represented by money – out of nowhere and yet the statistics show that >70% of them go bankrupt within 2 years. Why is that? Because they do not have the education necessary to handle that amount of power. Their progress is not even zero, it is negative.

The power that – I hope – you received from this book may not be "cold hard cash", but it is everything you need to generate that if this is what you want in life. This is not a joke and I am not even exaggerating. It is the power to make people do what you want them to do. It is the power to obtain things that seem impossible to have at the moment. It is the power to **get the most out of life.** Yet it is not enough.

As I said before, if you do want to accomplish any of the things I listed above, power alone is not going to cut it. You will have to educate yourself in order to use that power the way it should be used, otherwise all the techniques and talking tricks that you learned will never give you the maximum amount of satisfaction and progress.

From now on it is your duty to educate yourself and decide how you will use that power, since I cannot tell you anymore what you should do with it. What I can tell you instead is what I consider to be the most important and ethical rule that you must follow in every negotiation and generally in life: **ALWAYS AIM FOR A WIN-WIN SITUATION.**

This is the foundation of every true major success that you can and will have in life. It is what made people rich (not restrained to money) and **kept** them that way. If you aim for that in everything you do, I guarantee it will work for you too. **There is no queue in becoming successful.**

You may be wondering why this is so important. You may think about it like "Well... my product/service is worth $50, but why shouldn't I lie a little bit and maybe sell it for $100. I will never see the buyer again anyway so I should take advantage of that". Wrong!

The answer to that question is "people". You should not do that because of people. Most of us underestimate how small the world actually is and how big the communication networks between people are today. Information is spreading faster than ever before and it will keep on getting faster. This is why you **must never** think like that. Even if you are right and you will not see that buyer again, you will most likely see and deal with someone that he knows. Keep in mind that this applies to every person out there, so in my opinion screwing someone over just to get more than you deserve is simply a very bad idea. I will let you decide for yourself, but remember to always think at what can happen next.

However, if you decide to listen to my advice *and* aim for win-win situations, you will see amazing results over time. One happy prospect today can bring you one hundred new clients tomorrow, just like one disappointed prospect can and will cancel many deals for you. We see this happening every day around us, but we do not always pay attention to it.

When I was in high school (not a long time ago) I needed a math tutor and I was lucky enough to find probably the best one in town. She was recommended to me by a friend and after I finished highschool with an A+ in maths I also recommended her to some of my younger mates. A few weeks later, she called to thank me for the recommendation I made as some of my friends started working with her, but in reality she deserved it anyway and I was the thankful one. Do you see how one happy "client" can lead to a chain of buyers and good relations? I won something there (a good service in exchange for my money) and she won something as well (even more clients). This is how the world should work.

On the other hand, I also remember when my family paid someone to make a piece of furniture for my brother's room and it turned out to be a piece of $#!&. The quality was not even near "acceptable" considering how much we paid him and he was also late on delivery. A few weeks later a neighbor wanted to hire the same guy and asked my father if he was any good. You probably can imagine my dad's response and how that man lost at least a client because he chose a win-lose situation that made him a few extra bucks or a couple of hours less of work. Also, I recently heard that he is out of business, which does not surprise me at all.

Those are just two out of countless examples that I can give and I am pretty sure you got many similar examples in your own life as well. I hope that now you understand why it is so much better for everyone if you pick the win-win alternative every time you can and why it does not mean you will lose anything if you do so.

Keep in mind that life is not really that short and it existed way before money did, so that should raise some questions the next time we think about what is truly important on this planet.

After all, money is just paper and we only end up with the people around us, so be careful about what you prioritize in life. This is what I've been told from a young age and even though deep in my mind I know it is mostly true, I chose to see it for myself and started doing the opposite of what I've been told. From my point of view, the only way you can learn that money does or does not mean "happiness" is to actually generate a ton amount of them and see for yourself.

It may be a mistake, but it is the kind of mistake that we all should make.

- Afterword -

If you managed to get this far and to finish reading this book, I want to congratulate you. Deciding to start is probably one of the hardest parts of this process, or at least it was for me, but most likely we aren't that different.

The story is pretty much the same for everyone: you dream big, parents tell you to get your stupid ideas out of your head and go to school, you listen to them because you are young and end up with a highschool or bachelor degree yet little to no information at all about the real world. I've been there.

In the end though, you probably get that well paid job and, if you are lucky enough (and by that I mean you don't live in the USA or some other countries where education isn't free), you probably get to actually keep the money for yourself instead of paying the university debt, so I guess that is a plus.

When you get to that point you may either get that "I'm getting my life together" feeling which I heard is nice, or you may realize that you hate your job and you don't like working in general so you start thinking about other options.

The good news? The good news is that no matter in which half you fall, one thing is certain: it can always be better. This is what you must have in your mind at all times: "I can do better than that". Of course, this "better" can mean different things for all of us — a higher place in the company's hierarchy, money, whistling without a whistle, conquering Mars (hello Mr. Musk)... you name it. It is imperative not to settle down, because once you do that you automatically failed. Well, that is of course if your "better" isn't to settle down, but to be frank that would be a horrible "better".

The truth is that while I still believe negotiation is one of the most important skills one can learn, life is often more about "knowing" stuff rather than "getting" stuff. This is why you have to keep learning, keep improving yourself, no matter how bad or good your life gets.

What to learn? I don't give a s#!t, EVERYTHING. Learn about turtles, animals in general, oceans, space, rocks, relationships, brain, philosophy, math, art, bombs, guns, computers, cars, plants, drugs, laws, religions, countries, personalities, clouds, history, privacy and this list can go on forever. I'm fairly certain that you have no clue how the device you are using to read this book works, or if you have the paperback then you probably don't have any idea how they turn trees into f#(%!ng paper – and this is perfectly fine. It is totally ok to not know stuff, as long as you don't stop learning and getting better. Never acquire that "I'll never use this" mentality. Are you a man? Then man up and go face that sewing kit. Are you a woman? Awesome, now own up to your independency and learn to change that tire. I hope you'll never have to, but you should know how to do it just in case.

Disappointing enough though, you probably won't become a genius after all this learning. It sucks, I know, but let me tell you this: life is both too short/long to be dumb.

Learn as much as you can and live your life while you do it. Like Adler – unfortunately not so famously – suggested, "you must dance every moment of your life". It's not wrong to have goals, but remember that you live in the present and remember to enjoy the journey, otherwise you will regret the destination.

You still don't know where to start? How about you learn about riddles and cryptography. While the second can become really complicated (yes, I'm talking math and programming here), the first is often fun and a great exercise for your brain.

As I suppose you already guessed, I had something in mind when I proposed that domain. You see, there is a little hidden riddle in this book that you already read but you didn't observe, so I challenge you to find it and solve it. I will give you the first clue, you must find the others. Did you notice some random italic letters throughout this book? Well, let's just say they were not random at all.

Good luck!

Glossary-ish
(more like clarifications)

[1] **Negotiation** – I defined it at the very beginning of this book and I also insisted on this fact whenever I had the chance, but I feel the need to include it here as well. So once again, whenever we talk about negotiation, even though some examples may be misleading, **we are not necessarily talking about money.** Remember, from a simple smile to where you want to eat with your partner, everything is negotiation.

[2] **Seller** – Not only the guy who has a product with a price on it. Every negotiation has a seller, and we established that negotiation is not only about money or products. The seller is the person trying to obtain something specific: information, a date, fulfillment, money, etc.

In reality, you are a seller multiple times a day and in a negotiation there can often be 2 or more sellers and zero buyers, from an objective point of view.

[3]: **Buyer** – Besides the usual meaning of the word ("the person who wants to acquire an item by paying for it"), in the negotiations that don't include money, the buyer is usually the dummy. It is the person used by the seller to get that specific "something".

However, given the fact that we all want the best for ourselves, you will rarely deal with someone who is purely a buyer – someone who doesn't want anything in return or simply doesn't care. This is the reason why most of the time in negotiations there are more sellers and zero buyers.

From a subjective point of view, we can say that the buyer is usually the person with whom you are negotiating.

[4]: **Utility-per-page** (or U/P) – A theoretical measure that you will not find on Google or in any other books because I invented it. It refers to the amount of useful information that you get from a book relative to the number of pages. Since information is a subjective concept, different people cannot rate different books using this measurement because not everyone will agree, but you can use it in order to "calculate" the true value of a book for yourself. I felt the need to introduce such a unit after reading a lot of books and noticing a major difference between the old and the contemporary writings. Basically, I observed an alarming decline in the usefulness of books over the years, regardless of genres. If you will read books that are over 50 years old – I cannot name them as I do not want to start any disputes, but you can find them very easily – you will be astonished by the amount of information that you can get in just a few dozen pages. The problem is that as you come closer to the present, you can see a linear drop in the amount of utility that each book has to offer. In my opinion, this terrible phenomenon has mostly commercial and editorial reasons. As we go further in time we see that these days books are more about money and less about actually teaching people to do certain stuff or simply entertaining them. It turned from a way of spreading information to a huge business. A multi-billion dollar industry. This is why most authors today are looking to spread two sentences of useful information over twenty book pages so the publisher can sell it for a higher price. After all, in the world of books, bigger is not just "better", right? Of course not, it is also more expensive. Because of this, readers are forced to waste more money and precious time in finding that "golden fish" (the useful information) in a "sea" of pointless chatter. The worst part is that it's only getting worse and nobody seems to do anything about it. The world will reach a point where we will have all the information possible yet we will lack basic knowledge about everything. Of course, there are exceptions to this phenomenon, but overall we have a major problem. I am not saying that every contemporary author is doing that "spread" in information. On the contrary, I've read some recently published books

that I found very valuable and with a high U/P. The problem is that such writings are becoming increasingly rare, and I am afraid that they are on the verge of extinction. In the end, I guess only time will tell.

www.ingramcontent.com/pod-product-compliance
Lightning Source LLC
Chambersburg PA
CBHW030939240526
45463CB00015B/726